RUDOLF BAHRO'S first published work, *The Alternative in Eastern Europe*, NLB 1978, was widely hailed as one of the most important critical analyses of 'actually existing socialism'. His other writings include a study of Beethoven: *Die nicht mit den Wölfen heulen*, and two collections of speeches and articles, *Socialism and Survival* and *Wahnsinn mit Methode*, which both appeared in 1982. Bahro has become internationally known as a political theorist and a leading figure of the West German Green movement. He currently lives in Bremen.

Rudolf Bahro

Verso

From Red to Green

Interviews with New Left Review

Translated by Gus Fagan and Richard Hurst

The three interviews collected in this volume were conducted in spring 1980, autumn 1981 and summer 1983. The interviewers were Perry Anderson (pts. 1 & 2), Fred Halliday (pts. 1 & 3) and Monty Johnstone (pts. 1 & 2).

First published 1984
© New Left Review and Rudolf Bahro 1984

Verso Editions and NLB
15 Greek Street London W1V 5LF

Filmset in Times by
Comset Graphic Designs, Singapore

Printed in Great Britain by
The Thetford Press
Thetford, Norfolk

ISBN 0 86091 060 1
　　　0 86091 760 6 (Pbk)

Contents

Part One

1
Early Years

Let us begin by talking about your early life. How much did the Third Reich affect the way you grew up?

A great deal. The Nazi regime, the war and the Soviet Army liberation shaped my political development in a way that would have been quite different if the history of Germany had taken another course. But let me begin at the beginning.

I was born in 1935 in a little watering-place called Bad Flinzberg, in the Silesian Isergebirge. It was not home for long, however, because when I was six—it must have been in 1942—we moved to the neighbouring district, Kreis Löwenberg. It was there that I went to school, but somehow we never quite became part of the community. My father came from a village called Treppeln, near Guben, some thirty miles south of Frankfurt-on-Oder—today it's on the border between the GDR and Poland—where he was born on a farm in 1901. He was the second youngest of five sons, and since he was the most intelligent, he was sent to the agricultural college. There was no really scientific training for agricultural workers at the time, but his knowledge of biology and economics was so much greater than that of the average farm-worker that, while still a young man in the 1920s, he was given a job supervising estates in south-east Brandenburg. Not being an ambitious or forceful man by nature, he was never made inspector for the whole of an estate but only had to check the work in the fields, or to see that proper care was being taken of the farmyard, the stables or the barns.

In 1933 he married and moved to Bad Flinzberg where my mother's parents, themselves from Upper Silesia, had bought a little

4

house. The young couple let three or four rooms because the house hadn't been paid off yet, and my father continued to work as an 'assistant milk controller'.

Was it an official job?

Yes, it formed part of the Nazi bureaucracy that controlled agricultural production. He had to ensure that the milk was not adulterated and that it contained the necessary fat content. Animal husbandry, of course, was important for German war preparations.

What were your father's politics?

I never actually discovered, because he was a basically non-political person right up to 1945. It may be of interest, however, that he came from a Protestant, Prussian farmstead sympathetic to the Kaiser.

Was the whole area Protestant?

Yes, except for the remarkable Catholic enclave of Neuzelle. It may sound a little unfair, but my mother and particularly my grandmother were simple folk, pious almost to the point of bigotry. My grandfather was not quite so extreme, but he had to accompany his wife every Sunday, and my father's eldest brother, who took over the farm, also went to church faithfully to please his mother, even after her death. There are two novels by Hans Fallada set in the 1920s which evoke the world to which my father belonged after he left agricultural college. One is called *Wolf among Wolves*. The other, *Little Man, What Now?* has a character who administers an estate and is unsure whether his proper place is at the head of the servants' table or at the bottom of the master's. This must have been my father's position, for he recognized the atmosphere when they televised *Little Man, What Now?* years later in the GDR.

Actually, my father retained none of his earlier Christian beliefs, adopting instead a kind of naive, pantheist identification of God and nature. One spring when I was ten or twelve, I talked with him about religion and he used the example of all the plants and trees that were starting to blossom. It was *Deus sive natura*, in Spinoza's phrase. He naturally believed that there was some higher purpose in life, but when I later severed my connection with the Protestant Church, it worried him because of his relatives, not because of any religious commitment.

As far as I can tell—he once hinted at something of the kind—my father's general attitude in the 1920s was patriotic and nationalist, with a typical lower-class antipathy towards the aristocracy. On the estates he had direct experience of class divisions and social cleavages, yet he always rejected the stereotype of the landowner as a tyrant with whip in hand, as portrayed in Kuba's film *Schlösser und Katen*.[1] The real situation was perhaps even worse: for although the aristocracy may have consciously pursued the class struggle, ruling the estates in a highly authoritarian manner, the farm workers certainly had no such awareness.

Anyway, there was nothing in my father's outlook or background that drew him to Nazism. He had a certain authority based upon expert knowledge, and indeed, after 1945, when he had already left the village, he was asked to go back and run the local agricultural combine. I remember from early childhood that he often went out in the Isergebirge on his bicycle—in winter even on skis—to check that the milk was being properly collected. Then in 1939 or 1940, he was promoted to senior inspector for the whole of Kreis Löwenberg. In 1942 he joined the Nazi Party, not out of enthusiasm, as some others did, but simply because he would otherwise have lost his job and been drafted into the army. So, he joined the Party and soon became responsible for milk production in two *Kreise*: Löwenberg and Lauban. That same year, we moved to a place called Bad Gerlachsheim, in Kreis Lauban, from where my father exercised supervisory functions over the junior inspectors who visited the farms.

How would you describe your father's general cultural background?

His whole family had been conditioned by the events that led up to the foundation of the Second Reich under Bismarck and Kaiser Wilhelm I. Although they thought less of Wilhelm II, even tracing the seeds of the First World War to his youthful inexperience, the whole atmosphere in the farmhouse, as my father sat down to play cards with his two older brothers, harked back to the years between the war against Denmark over Schleswig-Holstein and the Great War of 1914–18. That was when history had started, and all their books came from the same period. My most vivid political memory from childhood is the mood of depression which came over my family when we heard that Hitler had invaded Russia. I do not recall anything specific, but I can well imagine that my father's unease at the course of events was also rooted in the Bismarck tradition.

What are the chief impressions the war itself has left on you?

It must really have started in Gerlachsheim, where a shoe repairer used to lend me Nazi magazines about tank attacks, bombers and so on. My father had to complete long forms in various colours about milk yields, and I used to cut swastikas from the pink forms until he told me to stop because he needed them. But it was only a game as far as I was concerned—the kind all children play. Nazi ideas made no mark on me, as it was only after the war that I came across them as such.

Then I remember a farm run by a man who had come back from Brazil, not because he was a rabid Nazi but just because he felt he had to do his bit. He had Russian women working for him on the farm, and we used to talk about who would win the war. Naturally I said that Germany would, since I had been reading those Nazi magazines and listening to the radio. But even that was really an act of cowardice on my part. I had always been afraid of bigger boys and was the last one to be picked for any game of football. It was the same physical fear, rather than political reasons, which filled me with relief when the end of the war absolved me from joining the Hitler Youth. I only overcame that fear when I was about eighteen.

As the fighting drew closer, we could hear the Russian guns forcing a passage across the Oder near Breslau, a good 150 kilometres away. My aunt made her way to us from Breslau, where her husband had had to join the Home Guard. A month or so later, in February 1945, my father also joined the Home Guard and the rest of us were evacuated: my mother, my aunt, my younger brother, who was eighteen months younger than me, my sister, who was three years younger, and myself. They took us via Zittau and Warnsdorf to a place called Trebitsch in Czechoslovakia: a medium-sized town, as I remember it, about the same as Guben.

The Czech family on whom we were billeted was obviously not on the side of the Germans, but they treated us quite well when they saw we were only women and children. The whole thing was a valuable experience for me, since it took me away from my familiar surroundings at school and so on. Shortly before the surrender on 5 May we were moved to southern Bohemia, and I remember seeing a slogan scrawled on the wall of Trebitsch railway station: 'Roosevelt the war criminal is dead.' It was in a log cabin in beautiful countryside near Budejovice that we finally heard the news of Hitler's suicide.

There were a number of violent episodes as we were shunted from one place to the next: the soldier in charge of us was beaten up, and the Russians tried to rape my aunt. Both the Russians and the Czechs wanted to get us out of the country to prevent any further incidents, so they took us to Gmünd, on the Austrian border. But since the British, or maybe it was the Americans, would not allow us to cross, we were taken to Bratislava and directed to a train bound for Wiener Neustadt. My mother, my aunt and I climbed on board with our luggage, but while my mother was going back for the other two children, the train started and left them behind. I never saw my mother again, nor my brother and sister. They were sent back to Silesia and died of typhus soon afterwards, partly because the Poles refused to feed them.

Meanwhile, my aunt and I camped out in one of the Vienna railway stations—the Nordbahnhof, I think—and spent our time squashing lice. She was an awkward and pretty helpless person, like her husband. They had no children and found it hard to adapt to new circumstances.

I had some success begging round the houses in Vienna. One of my victims, a Dr Erwin Heller, had lost his own son in the war and responded sympathetically as I spun him a yarn about my poor little sister, the death of my father in a U-boat, and so on. Indeed, a few years later this Dr Heller wrote and invited me to Austria, offering to pay for my studies with the idea that I should eventually take over his textile firm. The only reason I didn't accept was that I was so ashamed of having deceived him. He'd seen through me, of course, because no sister of mine had ever turned up at his house.

What happened to you after Vienna?

Well, somehow we found ourselves spending six months in a British prisoner-of-war camp in Carinthia. Then they tried to get us into American-occupied Bavaria, but we were turned back near Rosenheim and put in a refugee camp. Although the food and conditions were rather bad, we managed to survive and I don't remember being all that hungry.

In the spring of 1946 my aunt and I found ourselves on a farm in Eckelshausen, on the River Lahn in Hessen. Then my aunt learned that her husband was living in Erfurt, so we moved to the Soviet Zone and I travelled on back to Treppeln. My father was then staying with one of his brothers near Osnabrück, but he returned to Treppeln in the autumn of 1946, two months after me, and took over the farm that he ran until 1950.

Throughout 1947–48 I shared in all the ploughing, harrowing and other work. The only thing I was too small for was the mowing, although I was so afraid of the cow that I never milked it well. I came to feel my father's resentment at the compulsory delivery of all his milk—a necessary measure in those times of shortage, of course, in order to prevent the development of a black market. But I myself never went short of milk or anything else.

I remember one particular incident from this time. My friends and I used to make bows and arrows out of reeds and bits of elderberry bushes, and then go shooting in the fields around the church. One day the Bürgermeister caught us and told my father that it was very wrong to play with weapons like that. People laugh at it today, but that sort of attitude has left its mark on the development of the GDR.

You mentioned earlier your break with the Church. How did that come about?

I have very few memories from the time at Gerlachsheim—only the text of a sermon which I couldn't understand, 'The Word became Flesh and dwelt among us', from St John's Gospel. After the war, the nearest pastor was in Fünfeichen, seven kilometres away, and we used to go there for confirmation classes. But what we really enjoyed was the walk across the fields, which gave us the opportunity to throw stones at the earthenware insulation caps on the electricity cables. However, I soon began attending school in the town of Fürstenberg—now Eisenhüttenstadt—where a central school had been set up to replace all the little village schools, with their multi-age classes. The pastor who took the confirmation lessons in Fürstenberg was a rather unsympathetic type, more Catholic than Protestant, a lean and very upright man. It was the sort of situation described in Ehm Welk's novel *Die Heiden von Kummerow*,[2] as in the books by Fallada I mentioned.

I found the dogmatic tone of those classes very unpleasant: 'Thou shalt love and fear the Lord thy God...' and so forth. And it was made even worse by the woman, some forty years old, to whom we had to recite the Lutheran Catechism. She was the kind of person who lives only for the thought of salvation and never stops talking of the sufferings of Christ. As far as I was concerned, the last straw was when she told us the story of the Seven Wise Virgins who preserved their oil and the Seven Foolish Virgins who didn't. We all burst out laughing.

Anyway, I told my father I ought to leave the confirmation classes because I no longer believed it all. At the confirmation service itself, there was a boy with huge holes in his socks which showed when he knelt at the altar. This immediately gave me a fit of the giggles. When I eventually broke with the Church, however, this seemed an even bigger step than my simultaneous decision to join the Socialist Unity Party (SED).

Could we go back for a moment to your father's development. How did he relate to the new regime?

He joined the Farm Workers Party (*Demokratische Bauernpartei Deutschlands*) in 1950 and increasingly approved of things as the years went by. He had to play his part in the collectivization programme, but although he knew from experience that large-scale agriculture was more efficient, he was also aware that his two brothers in the next village, like all private farmers, did not want to give up what they had. This dichotomy made him particularly useful to the state, because he was trusted more than the Party officials who just came from the city to lay down the line. He addressed the farmers not so much in political terms as in the manner of: 'Well, it's going to come anyway, and you can't avoid it.' When they said it was only because the Russians were there, he replied that of course the Russians were there and it would be better to carry out the collectivization in their own way.

There were two main reasons why my father supported the GDR: one was the economic progress in agriculture; the other was his belief that everything which the Russians opposed, and which the Americans might support, was dangerous and could lead to war. This became particularly clear in 1968, when he tried to convince me that the invasion of Czechoslovakia was the right course—not on the basis of any concrete political argument, but simply out of support for the Russians. This was the first time we did not see eye to eye, and although I never told him all my ideas, it was not possible to pretend that nothing had changed. He found this unacceptable, his loyalty to the GDR being based on the old idea that one does not oppose the powers that be. His whole background in the Wilhelmine age and the Bismarck tradition, together with his experience of the big agricultural estates, made him prefer the type of state represented by the GDR. Having been through the Kaiser's Germany, then the chaos of the Weimar Republic, then Hitler and the war, he naturally found the GDR the best—and certainly better than the Federal Republic. So did my mother.

But didn't you say she died of typhus in 1946?

My stepmother, I should have said. My father got married again in 1950, to a working-class woman. Her father had been a Social Democrat and a trade unionist, a bargee on the canals whose life had been about as far removed as one could get from the world of the Prussian Junkers. He had lived through the 1920s, although by then he was an old man, no longer politically active or interested in the Socialist Unity Party. My stepmother was more rigid than my father in religion and such matters, but they didn't occupy her thoughts very much and the couple got on well together.

My half-brother had a typical GDR career. He trained as a locksmith, then took an engineering course and worked for a time in a junior position at the Central Economic Planning Division in Berlin.

He joined the Party rather too late to avoid losing his job there, and so he had to take a lower-paid one elsewhere. He didn't join out of conviction, nor was it just a matter of furthering his job prospects—as people often argue is the case—but rather of adapting to the new circumstances. Not that I had anything against it, but it is the kind of thing that worries you in any society.

How did your own political ideas mature after 1945?

My first memory of events with a directly political significance is my father's account of how my mother, sister and brother had died after being deprived of food by the Poles. This naturally affected the way I thought for a while, especially since our house in Treppeln was only seven or eight kilometres from the Oder border with Poland. In Fürstenberg I used to go with my step-grandfather to fetch hay from the banks of the river. As we clambered over the grass-covered stone groynes that jutted into a narrow part of the river, I always had the feeling that we ought to cross over on account of my mother. Then there was the influence of two of my schoolteachers in particular, who were opposed to developments in East Germany from what we would call a petty-bourgeois point of view, although I don't know to what extent they were infected with Nazi ideas. So, up to the time I left school I suppose I was politically against the way things were going in the country.

Were you in the Pioneers, the Communist children's organization?

No, I wasn't, I'm proud to say. At the beginning the Pioneers were like the cooperative farms—the worst joined first. The better pupils, those who came from better-class homes and had more chance of getting on, tended not to join. Fürstenberg had no real bourgeoisie: the population was overwhelmingly composed of smallholders, with just one capitalist firm, a few ship-owners, doctors, chemists and so on. Their children weren't in the Pioneers. And since I was pretty bright, nor was I.

Didn't the school put pressure on you to join?

I can't really remember. Maybe they said something to me. An older girl with whom I ran the school library tried to get me to join, but that was quite normal. I did reluctantly join the Free German Youth at secondary school, where the old-style headmaster assembled the new intake in 1950 and made it clear that this was the expected thing to do. What could I have done? It was the only time I felt under pressure to do something against my will.

But there were also a number of people who persuaded me to avoid any directly political involvement—my biology teacher, for instance, an impressive man who used to go for walks with me across the fields reciting passages from Goethe's *Faust*.

Shortly afterwards a new headmaster was appointed. Once a keen Nazi officer, he had changed his colours and joined the Socialist Unity Party. But he soon had to leave, partly because his previous activity became known and partly because he set about seducing the older girls.

Then there was a young teacher of twenty-three who had once been made leader in the Hitler Youth as a result of his sporting talent. He was a tough character, very different from me, with considerable powers of persuasion. He was a convinced Marxist and used to explain to us the contradictions in the political situation, never relaxing his ideological and political pressure, particularly on the brighter pupils. Once, when I was not unusually playing cops and robbers in my blue FDJ (*Freie Deutsche Jugend*—Free German Youth) shirt, he gave me a firm ticking-off for using the sacred garment for such profane purposes. On another occasion, he became very angry with me for quoting a line from Schiller about the majority being a meaningless entity. After he had been there about a month, he went into the classroom next to mine and wrote on the blackboard: 'Why are you all such hypocrites? Why are you so dishonest? Why don't you say what you think?' In other words: 'Why don't you tell me what you disagree with, so that I can have the chance to argue with you?'

This was 1950?

No, 1951. When I was in the ninth class, for children between fifteen and sixteen, he gave us lessons on Lenin's *State and Revolution* and naturally asked us for a definition of the state. We produced the standard answer that it is the instrument for controlling the affairs of society, but he retorted that for Lenin it is the instrument by which one class oppresses another. We gaped in amazement. Then one of us—it may have been me—asked whether this meant that some people were being oppressed in the GDR. Of course they are, he said.

I suddenly realized that in all the previous discussion about democracy, the people, and so on, the real issue had been a harsh power struggle in which certain people are held down. Our teacher next gave us a rather crude account of classes, and it was clear from the very first lesson that it wasn't just a matter of the opposition between workers and capitalists; that if a worker shared the capitalist ideology, he had to be put down as a source of help for the capitalists.

This was a key point in my development, and in 1952 I applied to join the Party. I became enthusiastic about primitive films like *The Unforgettable Year 1919*, in which Stalin holds the front at Petrograd and Bukharin is caricatured as a villain. There were also two well-known films about Ernst Thälmann, and a number of Russian films which painted an ideal picture of Russia similar to the one conveyed by Glinka's music. Above all, I remember reading the first volume of Mikhail Sholokhov's *Virgin Soil Upturned*, which brought out the conflicts in society with particular clarity.

Another crucial moment in my political education was the Third Youth Festival in 1952.

So you went to Berlin during this period?

Yes, but I spent most of the time in the Western part. Not that I had gone there with that intention: I was very much in two minds at the time. I remember the office of some religious organization near Witzleben Station in West Berlin. One of the anti-socialist publications on display was a rag called *The Tarantula*, which had on its cover a picture of Stalin driving a war chariot pulled by leaders of the other Communist states, with Mao as the biggest of the horses. That didn't make much of an impact on me. But I was affected by another of their publications: an autobiography by El Campesino.[3] I read it without understanding a great deal, but when I returned from Berlin, I hid it in the attic out of a kind of fear. I was not afraid of the police, but I did have a bad conscience towards Behrend, my teacher, and towards myself for having spent so much time in West Berlin.

Did Behrend know?

I don't think I ever told him—or if I did, it was only much later. Although I wasn't yet fully committed, I felt a certain obligation towards him and was perhaps afraid of landing in trouble. I didn't see the situation in its proper historical perspective at the time, and only when I read El Campesino again years later did I remember this earlier episode. Anyway *The Tarantula* pictured the very opposite of what I had experienced in 1952, and it was in September of that year that I applied to join the Party.

The Festival lasted three weeks, and for the first two I had to stay in Fürstenberg as an FDJ announcer at the railway station. During other holidays I used to work on the Eisenhüttenkombinat-Ost project, unloading bricks and repairing the railway tracks that continually broke under the weight of incoming supplies. Actually it has become the most attractive of the new towns in the GDR, set in a rolling landscape with the town on one side and the industrial complex on the other. Before I left the GDR, after coming out of prison, I went back to say goodbye to my stepmother and one of my old teachers.

Not Behrend?

No, no. He had died. He belonged to an unhappy generation which, having been forced to fight against the Russians, was more deeply affected by the Nazi period than we were. He was drummed out of the school because of an affair with a girl, but his downfall was also partly caused by the fact that he had once improved his lot by supporting the Nazi regime. Prospects for men of his generation are hopeless in the GDR, and it made all the difference to be just a few years younger. Another point, of course, was that the older generation, already disillusioned by their experience under Hitler, were not so shocked by the denunciation of Stalin in 1956.

Was Stalin's death an important event for you?

Yes, and it was at least an experience for all the other pupils. I recited

Johannes R. Becher's lofty poem at school: *Als es geschah an jenem 5 März und leise, immer ferner schlug sein Herz*, and so on. We stood there with tears in our eyes and the flag at half mast, mounting a guard of honour with air rifles in front of Stalin's portrait and wondering how life could go on. Some months later, during my last year at school in January 1954, I put together a speech in praise of Lenin from the history of the CPSU, spiced with quotations.

But after Stalin's death came the uprising of 17 June in East Berlin. What effect did that have on you?

It didn't impress me deeply, because I was so conditioned that I immediately saw it as the counter-revolution. I watched the workers from Eisenhüttenstadt march past the school-gate, and I may even have broken school regulations to get a better view outside. Two things stick in my mind. One was the rumour that some of the blast-furnacemen who opposed the government were prepared to throw people into the fire if the works were attacked. The other is the behaviour of the local Party secretary. At the district Party meetings I was allowed to attend as secretary of the FDJ, he had given two or three speeches that made a strong impression on me. But on 17 June, from what I heard, he simply broke down and took to his heels. That's all I can recall about the 17th of June.

Were there any demonstrations or shooting incidents?

No, there was only one confrontation in front of Fürstenberg Town Hall. I should mention that the development of the giant industrial complex at Eisenhütten East was a crucial backdrop to these events.[4]

What was your attitude to so-called dissidents like Zeiser and Rudolf Hernstadt?

At the time I believed what the Party newspaper *Neues Deutschland* said. Hernstadt impressed me as a speaker, and I remember his intervention at the Second Party Congress in 1952 about building socialism and 'stamping our will on the course of events'. But it never occurred to me that the Party could be wrong.

Was there any discussion of such matters?

To some extent, but I can't really remember. I was on a school holiday by the Baltic Sea when I read about it, and the history teacher in charge of us was probably not very frank. Besides, I'm sure I wouldn't have trusted him much.

You were at school when the events of 17 June took place. Were there discussions among your fellow-pupils or with your teachers?

We became increasingly analytical throughout my time at secondary school. In my own class four or five took something like the Party line, while about the same number were hostile to it, and those in the middle tended to side with the strongest. Some of us, including myself on occasion, would shout down our opponents, but discussions were always going on. Although I did not realize it then, my views eventually won the day because the whole apparatus of power was behind me.

Were you allowed to read books from the West on the history and theory of Marxism? Or was everything very strictly controlled?

Yes, it was. But there's more to it than that. As a schoolboy I was always concerned with the broader problems of society. My stepmother, with her Social Democratic background, had a strange mixture of books: for instance, there was an edition of Schiller's poems with an introduction by Franz Mehring, then Thomas Mann's *Buddenbrooks* and Goethe's *Faust* alongside sentimental novels and other lightweight stuff. She also had nationalist novels like Ernst von Salomon's *Die Geächteten* (*The Outlawed*) and other books that glorified the 'German spirit'. Very soon after the war, I read Felix Dahn's *Ein Kampf um Rom* and a few out-and-out reactionary books, one of them a story by a man called E. von Mahlzahn attacking the French Revolution and another in very similar vein on the Russian Revolution. I didn't fully understand their historical import at the time, of course, any more than I did that of the El Campesino. It was a pretty mixed bag—though even these reactionary books were well written, rather in the style of Gustav Freytag. Then, following Behrend, I turned to Marx, Lenin's *Materialism and Empirio-Criticism* and Engels's *Anti-Dühring*.

What Marx did you read?

The Communist Manifesto, Wage-Labour and Capital, Wages, Price and Profit—the simplest things to start with.

What about the political texts?

I only read those at university. Most of the older schoolteachers were discharged after 1945, and the younger ones were really students whose studies had been interrupted by the war—people of above-average education from semi-bourgeois families, not tainted by Nazism. Several of them were people of real quality. The one I went to say goodbye to—an ex-major from Bavaria called Heinz-Lutz von Hauenschild—was the sort of man who would have joined the Nationalkommittee Freies Deutschland during the war.[5] He later became a member of the National Democratic Party in the GDR, but he was very different from all those who joined the Party with a closed mind, people like Comrade Wunschgetreu[6] in Strittmatter's novel *Ole Bienkopp*, who is upright and moral by his own lights but just does what is required of him. This Hauenschild was an excellent speaker who had studied a certain amount of German literature and taught us Classical authors like Lessing, Goethe and Schiller, together with Thomas Mann's *Buddenbrooks* and Heinrich Mann's *Henri Quatre* novels—my favourites. I also read Romain Rolland's *Jean Christophe*.

But wasn't Rolland too pacifist in tone?

I don't know about that, but his works were published in the GDR. The longest essay I ever wrote in school was on Heinrich Mann's *Henri Quatre*. For my abitur I wrote on Georg Herwegh—again part of that bourgeois-democratic tradition.

Another of my teachers, from whom I gained a new perspective on religious questions, was a clergyman's son who had studied physics and was something of a musician. He used to play the organ in his father's church on Sundays and conducted the school choir in which I sang for four years. We used to sing folk-songs and choruses from Weber's *Freischütz*, but he was also obliged to do political songs in praise of Stalin, proletarian ideals and so on. It was he, by the way, who introduced me to Beethoven; and in 1953, on the 125th anniversary of Schubert's death, Hauenschild got me to give two accompanying talks to recitals of the composer's songs and chamber music by amateur musicians from Fürstenberg.

The other man was a first-rate teacher of physics and mathematics, and it was thanks to him that I got good marks in maths. A stimulating, individualist type of person, his ideal in life was to earn enough summer money selling ice-cream on the Baltic to spend the rest of the year painting and doing other things he liked. His worldview was based on Einstein, so that when we challenged his beliefs— I was reading *Materialism and Empirio-Criticism* at the time and was convinced I knew the precise nature of objective reality—he used to tell us about the theory of relativity. All in all, these school years were a very profitable period for me.

I felt that I wanted to study something 'cultural' at university, and so I went to Leipzig for some reason and presented myself at the Department of Philosophy. There was a secretary there with 'Parson's Wife' written all over her face. (It's unkind of me to say such a thing, especially as I didn't know her at all, but she had that sort of churchy look about her.) When I timidly enquired whether I could study there, she solemnly rose to her feet and boomed out that this was Leipzig, and that the professor of philosophy was no less a person than Ernst Bloch. That was the end of Leipzig for me. I went to study philosophy in the very different atmosphere of Berlin.

As it happened, this proved to be a fortunate choice, especially as the Stalinist opposition to Bloch later became far more unpleasant than anything we experienced in Berlin. The philosophy courses had only started two years before, and we were the first students with a proper abitur. Those ahead of us were a good deal older and more mature, but we were all loyal to the Party and, with some exceptions, became or already were members. One belonged to the old Social Democratic Party, which remained legal in the GDR until 1959, while others were members of the Liberal or other parties. However, they were being groomed for jobs in their respective organizations, and were therefore basically on the side of the SED. Many Party members were only starting to read Marx for themselves, and it was more a question of laying the foundations than of gaining access to the kind of books on Marxism you asked me about earlier. Your question only really becomes relevant in the 1960s.

There were a number of weighty figures on the university staff: Georg Klaus, who was working on cybernetics but lectured on logic; Klaus Zweiling, whose lectures I did not have to attend so often but whom I knew from Party meetings as a man with fire in his belly, although perhaps a little repetitive; and Hermann Scheler, who was said to have belonged to the Socialist Workers Party that Willy Brandt helped to found. Zweiling had belonged to another of those splinter groups, but I don't remember which one. Although we knew little about such past history, we could all feel that these were personalities in their own right.

The various assistants came from the wartime generation and were mostly of inferior calibre. One of the better ones was Erich Hahn, who is now a leading philosopher in the GDR. He was only slightly older than us and had just finished his own studies, although he wasn't very concerned with internal politics, as I recall. Another I wanted to mention was Walter Besenbruch, a real old-style Communist who lectured on aesthetics. He had spent ten years in a Nazi concentration camp, and this seemed to have affected his concentration, making his lectures rather confused. But all these old Communists were absolutely sincere in their way. Kurt Hager's lectures on the history of Marxist philosophy gave me some knowledge of the Social Democratic movement—his source was probably Franz Mehring's *History of German Social Democracy*.

The only occasion on which the whole level dropped was when they sent us a former Russian polar aviator, a Comrade Professor Kozlovski, to give us a lecture on dialectical materialism. He called his talk a *Lehrvorlesung* but I wrote it on the blackboard as *Leervorlesung*.[7] As a result I was pulled up and told that it was very improper to treat a Soviet comrade in that way, a man who had fought against Hitler and whom our Soviet friends had sent to help us.

In general, however, we received a very sound basis of knowledge, and I'm not sure that students today get anything better. I also read things for myself, of course, like Kuno Fischer's *History of Modern*

Philosophy. What we never encountered was a critique of Marxism, as opposed to pre-digested rejection of all such criticism. When you read Marx for yourself or look at his correspondence with Engels, you realize that, despite his authoritarian character, the anti-authoritarian spirit of his writings inevitably brings them into conflict with the reality of the bureaucratic process. As long as I was at university, there was a kind of theological pressure that prevented the real facts from making themselves felt. Some of my fellow-students were certainly passing information to the security police, as I later discovered at my trial, and the whole atmosphere was very similar to that which Zdenek Mlynař described among Czech students in Moscow. The real situation in the country only became apparent when I went to work in the lignite fields or toiled away helping the inefficient collective farms to bring in their autumn potato harvest.

How many students were there in your group?

About twenty—perhaps more. There were between 150 and 200 in the Philosophy Department, at least a hundred of them in the Party.

Did you read any books at all that were opposed to Marxist philosophy?

Not really. Everything we needed to know was supposedly contained in the approved sources: information about Dühring in Engels's *Anti-Dühring*, for example. At some point I must have read Nietzsche, but not any strictly anti-Marxist literature.

Did people read Lukács?

Yes. *The Destruction of Reason* and his book on the young Hegel.

Were his works published in the GDR?

Yes, of course: his book on Thomas Mann, his essays and so on. As a student, I must have read at least as much classical German literature as I did Marx and Engels, above all writers in the humanist tradition like Feuchtwanger, Thomas Mann, Heinrich Mann, Hermann Hesse.

Anna Seghers?

Not very much. She's not such a great figure, for me at least. Then there was Döblin.

Remarque?

Not until later. I didn't find him so important.

Brecht?

Again, not until later. For me it was not Brecht but Becher who occupied the centre of the stage. And Weinert, of course. But I found the literature of the bourgeois age important as well, down to Hofmannsthal. I was very fond of Rilke, and I went to plays and concerts in Berlin. The whole period was a general education for me.

My special field was aesthetics, or rather literature. I followed lectures by Kantorowicz (who later went to the West) and others on early twentieth-century literature, Expressionism, poets like Trakl and so on. Havemann was lecturing at this time, but he was already a controversial figure. Although real Party members like myself were not supposed to attend, we got the gist of what was going on. The whole of Humboldt University in Berlin was an ideological battleground in the 1950s. We were sent to West Berlin to recruit for the Socialist Unity Party, and once we found ourselves in West Germany with the utterly delusory mission of giving indirect support to the SPD.

Where did you go?

To Dusseldorf and Mönchengladbach. When I was in West Berlin, I didn't change a single East German mark or go to a single film. Once I went with a friend of the family from Treppeln to see Büchner's *Dantons Tod* in the Schillertheater, but even then I had a bad conscience.

Did you read Ernst Bloch at this time?

Yes, but only his book on Hegel. I also heard him lecture once on Hegel shortly before he left the GDR. I didn't really experience him to the full, although I felt an affinity with what he called the Principle of Hope. (His book on this theme was actually lying on my desk when they came to arrest me.) Later I read his *Spirit of Utopia*, I think, and his book on Thomas Münzer. I read a great deal during my student days, most of it outside the curriculum. Then, in 1956, came the great crisis over the denunciation of Stalin.

2
From 1956 to 1968

What impact did the 20th Congress of the CPSU have on you?

My first reaction to Khruschev's speech was that it couldn't be right to treat Comrade Stalin in that way.

Was that the general view among Party members at the university?

I wouldn't say so. It was the reaction of the youngest and most naive among us. At school we had had Lenin's picture on the wall, not Stalin's, and I could feel the difference in quality between their writings. But I never played one off against the other.

Was Khruschev's report read out?

No. We could read it for ourselves—not the secret speech, that is, but the official report discrediting Stalin.

But wasn't the official report actually read out at certain Party meetings?

Well, enough information reached us anyway. Hannes Hörnig, who is now in charge of the scientific department of the SED Central Committee, used to come to Party meetings in the Philosophy Department in order to explain the line. I always found him reasonable and approachable. What annoyed me was not the report itself but the way Ulbricht presented it. Without any kind of explanation he suddenly declared that Stalin was no longer to be reckoned among the classics of Marxism. When I heard this, I immediately thought of a quote from Nietzsche's *Zarathustra*: 'As I lay there and slept, a sheep came and ate the laurel wreath from off my head, and said: "Lo, Zarathustra is no longer a philosopher!"' I sprang this on some friends during a lecture break and they all burst out laughing. There were no unpleasant consequences, because at that time the Party didn't have the power to deal with such trivial incidents. It wasn't even mentioned during my interrogation in 1977, so perhaps no one ever reported it.

I considered the situation in Poland and Hungary to be of special importance. At the time of the Russian intervention in Hungary, I put up an article on the departmental notice-board to the effect that since we trusted the Party, the Party should also trust us and tell us the truth about Hungary and, above all, Poland. I was hauled over the coals for this, but one of my comrades helped me to save my skin by telling me that I was just out to make myself a martyr, and that I should forget about it. As time went by, however, the lower echelons found it more and more necessary to conceal things from those at the top, and the man who helped me was himself later in trouble for siding with Havemann.

Although the whole thing eventually blew over, it had become clear that Comrade Bahro was not as reliable as they had thought. Indeed, in private discussion a number of us even posed the question of how to get rid of Ulbricht in order to rescue socialism in the GDR.

Was this before or after the events in Hungary?

After.

But before the arrest of Wolfgang Harich?

Yes. I had a group of friends—certainly not the least intelligent among the students—who shared the same ideas. The problem was not the structure of the Party but freedom of opinion within the Party, freedom to discuss, free access to information, combined with the conviction that Ulbricht had to be removed.

Ulbricht seems to have been a very negative figure for you.

It's not quite as simple as that. By 1957 I had come round to the view that, given the circumstances in Germany, Ulbricht had been right to close ranks as he did. No doubt I was manipulated in this direction, but we were anyway very close to the Party line. The Party stabilized around Ulbricht chiefly because there had been a counter-revolutionary potential in Hungary, with Communists being hanged and so on. The issue became one of Party loyalty and Jesuit-type discipline.

But what effect did it have on you to discover that things in the Soviet Union were not as you had imagined, that crimes had been committed, and so on? Didn't that raise basic political and ideological questions?

No, not at the time.

Did you never manage to read the text of Khruschev's secret speech?

No. I only read the report to the 20th Party Congress, from which it emerged that Stalin was no longer viewed in the same light. You must remember that between 1952 and 1953 I would never have looked at a West German newspaper or listened to West German radio, not even to Beethoven. It just wasn't the done thing.

Nevertheless, the June 1956 resolution of the Central Committee of the CPSU, which deals with the period of the so-called 'personality cult', does refer to massive repressive measures under Stalin. Surely there couldn't have been any secret about them.

Well, all I can say is that I and most of my generation only came to learn of it bit by bit. There was a poem by Kuba and Louis Fürnberg called *Weltliche Hymne*, which summed it all up for us by warning that the imperialists were trying to blur the distinction between friend and foe in our own ranks. Stalin's crimes were yet one more reason for getting rid of imperialism, since there would have been no need for them if imperialism had not existed. I cannot deny that I found parts of the argument convincing.

What significance did you attach to events in Poland?

They were basically dominated by events in Hungary, which were counter-revolutionary as far as I was concerned. I read things about the Polish priests and so on, but I wasn't yet so completely politicized that nothing escaped me. At that time, for example, I would probably have grasped the significance of events in Nicaragua but not of those in El Salvador.

What about Yugoslavia? Up to 1955 the Russians called Tito a fascist and an ally of the Americans. Then, in 1955, Khruschev went to Yugoslavia and everything changed: Rajk's 'confessions' had been false, Kostov should never have been tried, and so on. It had a shattering effect on us here to learn that what we had believed—not about Communism as such but about the nature of the Communist system—was wrong.

It had the same effect on me, and I wrote a number of poems about it. But I still believed that the imperialists had basically engineered the situation by planting agents in our midst and converting Beria into their direct or indirect tool. Who could tell whether German intelligence had not been involved in those groups of Germans about whose fate under Stalin we sometimes heard? As in the poem by Kuba and Fürnberg, everything was both admitted and justified. In 1965 or so, when I was deputy editor of the magazine *Forum*, I discussed the Russian Revolution for three whole days with the critic Alfred Kurella, who defended Stalinism without concealing the show trials or anything else. Although I didn't fully accept what he said, I conceded his right to see things that way. As for Ulbricht, I had stopped seeing things in terms of personalities by the time I read Isaac Deutscher's biography of Stalin. That was in 1965 or 1966.

And you were able to get that in the GDR?

I got it from a Swiss Communist who was living there. It demonstrated that Stalin's rise was an inevitable process which had little or nothing to do with the individual personality. Wilhelm Pieck was a remarkable exception to this, in that he displayed an unusual degree of humanity.

Let's move on to two other key events during your years as a student at the Humboldt University in Berlin. One is the fall of Bulganin and Malenkov in 1957; the other is the second crisis within the SED itself, associated with the Schirdewan group.

Both of these appeared as peripheral events whose meaning was not altogether clear. Naturally I was aware that arguments were going on, but I took them to be natural consequences of the 20th Party Congress. In 1960, when I was in Greifswald, I remember fully agreeing with an article by Khruschev in *Neues Deutschland* which argued that, if we were to go forward, we had to put our hesitations on one side and face the problems before us.

Any differences I had were more of a theoretical nature. For example, I was of the opinion that Lenin's concept of matter was not monistic, and that consciousness must be matter if the world was to have a unity. It was on such questions that I showed myself to have a mind of my own that was not yet ready to be put through the Party mill. Feeling that it was necessary to take the long way round, I therefore agreed to take over the editorship of a village paper in the Oderbruch, north of Frankfurt-on-Oder. If I had taken the short route to a university career, I would probably have become a conventional *apparatchik*. I once wrote a poem in honour of Khruschev in which I used a phrase that nothing should count except the force of the argument, but that kind of attitude was incompatible with Party discipline. Even at the time when I was appointed deputy editor of *Forum*, it was still this basic non-conformity of my character which prevented me from becoming a typical Party bureaucrat.

Was your attitude to Khruschev positive or negative at this time?

I have always taken a positive view of Khruschev, in spite of all the justifiable criticism one could level at him. I regard him as the most courageous man in the recent history of the Soviet Union. He was also, perhaps, the most human—not in the sense of humanistic, but as a rounded man with the courage to live out his own personality, with remarkably little heed to bureaucratic protocol, while never ceasing to be accessible to others. It has to be said that once the old guard of the Marxist-Bolshevik tradition had been shot, he did what was possible with his semi-reform. There was a certain subjectivism about him, and he naturally didn't go far enough, but no one went any further. Brezhnev represents a return to Stalinism, a reassertion of the power of the Party apparatus.

Would you say that what happened in the GDR *after the 20th Congress of the* CPSU *was not a liberalization but, on the contrary, a strengthening of the process of centralization, both politically and economically?*

Yes, and I went along with it, I must admit. Since Ulbricht was not disgraced in 1956 but actually consolidated his position, it was logical that that should happen. The people as such had no say in the matter, and he was able to get the whole Party apparatus to rally behind him against those who had caused difficulties in 1956. The whole Khruschevite experience was little more than a surface adjustment in the GDR, confined to theoretical discussions in philosophical journals and other peripheral contexts. It was clear that Ulbricht was firmly in charge and that things were going to stay that way for some time.

I should add that I have never concerned myself with the history of the Socialist Unity Party, and what I have been giving are impressions and opinions. It would be wrong for me to imply that I have been passing scientific judgements, because I don't know how the inner mechanism of the Party was working at the time.

It is easy to forget that in the GDR—unlike Poland, for example—the existence of the Federal Republic always posed the danger of a putsch. This made opponents of Ulbricht hesitate much longer, and placed people like Harich in a rather weak position.

Is that still true today?

Of course. It was my problem too, and still is to some extent. Had I stayed in the GDR and aligned myself with Havemann, for example, I would have become a target for those on both sides who continue to wage the cold war.

At this point, may we ask you what you learnt at Humboldt University about the history of the Communist movement in Germany. Did you know about the early problems of the Communist Party, the March Action, October 1923, the sharp divisions between the SPD and the KPD?

Thälmann was presented to us as a sacred figure almost like Stalin, while the Hamburg revolt in 1923 was simply a heroic act, full stop. The only criticism, already stated in 1935, was that the united front policy came too late, but even this point was never thought through to the end. We were always referred to Thälmann's assessment from jail that although the German Communists had their share of blame, it was much less than in everyone else's case.

What about Stalin's purges of the KPD in 1939 and 1940? Under Ulbricht, of course, nobody was shot or put on trial.

That's right. There are no corpses at the bottom of our garden, as they used to say.

But was it known that Stalin had had members of the KPD murdered?

Yes, we knew. But you must remember that people weren't sure how much of it was propaganda or the work of Western agents. Our lecturers certainly did not welcome discussion of past mistakes, preferring to talk about the establishment of socialism in the GDR and the great tasks ahead. Ideological questions only interested a certain section of the Party, and even they were of necessity chiefly occupied with practical matters. People used to say: 'Come on, comrades, let's stop talking about the past and get on with the job!' In the GDR the Party is responsible for everything, even the smallest detail of economic planning. It's the Party's responsibility if the economic plan goes wrong, so that if a particular spare part for a machine, say, is suddenly delivered in large quantities, it is a more important event than the Russian intervention in Afghanistan. A short report would be given at the beginning of the Party meeting, explaining in the terms of the official communiqués how Soviet troops had been forced to intervene because of the threat of an imperialist invasion, how the imperialists were out to encircle the Soviet Union, how Western bases were located to that end, and so forth. Any questions? That's the way it went.

So there would be no critical discussion of such matters within the Party?

They would be discussed only in small circles of members who trusted one another and knew that nothing would go into the Party files. Even then, no one could be sure that it would not reach the State Security. When something is reported, the person in question is not called to account, but the information is stored for possible future reference. Although it is not as common as people think, a group of, say, seven close members might contain one who reports on their discussion. Above all in intellectual circles, there is one individual with a weak spot who can be used as an informer. This does not happen so much in offices and factories: I used to be pretty outspoken in my own little group, but outside people hardly knew how much my views deviated from the Party line.

Let us come now to your experiences in agriculture.

When I was sent to Seelow, in the Oderbruch, to edit the village newspaper, I came under an SED district divided into a number of sub-districts; my own one was called Sachsendorf and consisted of seven fairly large villages. The paper was called *The Line*—a fortnightly printed on eight sides of A4. It was as sharp as a razor, I can tell you.

I was particularly glad to be there during the period of collectivization, between autumn 1959 and summer 1960. The telephone in the office of the local Party secretary had to be manned day and night, and I remember that once, when I was on night duty, his wall sported an area map on which certain villages were marked as not playing their full part in the drive.

So some of the farmers resisted collectivization?

It couldn't really be called resistance, because the state was too powerful and the farmers knew there was no escape. But whenever someone proved stubborn, a Party official would visit the farm and go through the same routine. Who's afraid of collectivization? Do you believe those stories about collectives being inefficient? If you're in favour of peace, you must join.

Are you talking of people who had been given land in the 1945 Land Reform or of those who had owned land before?

There were both in the Oderbruch, but those who had worked on the big estates showed a greater inclination to join the collectives.

And now, twenty years later, do you think the farmers would leave the collectives if they could?

That question has been completely overtaken by history. They're far better off now than they were then.

But that doesn't necessarily mean they're satisfied with the situation.

I'd put it this way. The older generation who couldn't reconcile themselves to losing their farm are now dead. The younger ones—those still on the land—have taken on specific functions within the collectives and become integrated into the system. After some early discrimination, even the large-scale farmers have discovered new fields of activity and often become dominant figures again.

Nevertheless, I always considered it unfortunate that collectivization took many of the decisions out of the hands of the actual producers, thereby depriving them of an overall view of the situation. And despite the increase in productivity, my view has been confirmed by the resulting ecological problems.

It would seem that, while the process of collectivization has been far from satisfactory in Russia and Poland, it has proved a considerable success in the GDR. Why should there be this difference?

There are a number of reasons. First, most farmers had been in the army and knew there was no point in fighting something that the Soviet Union was determined to push through. What they really wanted was a proper law establishing the system of collectivization which would put an end to the arbitrariness and psychological pressure. My uncle Emil, for instance, was willing to give up his farm but couldn't bring himself to do so when he thought of the family tradition and all that his father had built up. If there had been a proper law, the problem would have been non-existent and everything would have become much easier. Secondly, with the possible exception of Czechoslovakia, the GDR was the only East European country where the numerical relationship between town-dwellers and country-dwellers was to the disadvantage of the latter. Since the towns were so well developed, it was possible for us to combine collectivization with technological progress in agriculture. Finally, the whole process was carried out like a military operation, in which the Party was in a strong position to exert pressure and production was at no time interrupted or impaired. There were a few cases of suicide, but that was inevitable. In the end it became a pressure of numbers, as more and more were forced into the collectives. But there was very little physical coercion—unlike in the Soviet Union, where collectivization virtually became a civil war.

I can't say for certain whether there were any arrests. If a farmer set his dog on the 'collectivizer' when he came, I can imagine that this would have been considered resistance to the arm of the law and that the farmer would have been dealt with accordingly. But although my job in Seelow mostly cut me off from the population, I think I can say that such events were not common.

How long did the operation last, all told?

The campaign for total collectivization only lasted some six months, between 1959 and 1960, starting in the area around Rostock. Of course, there had been isolated collectives in most villages since 1952.

How did you come to leave Seelow?

That was a typical affair. The collectivization drive was dominated by a number of powerful figures who, from an economic point of view, played a progressive role, especially since the first collectives usually brought in the poorer and more backward farmers. However, there was one such man who made himself extremely unpopular by running the collective over their heads in an authoritarian manner. When he applied for a position in the Party headquarters at Frankfurt-on-Oder, I wrote to the local secretary that he had caused a great deal of trouble at a time when we needed to get the majority of people on our side. I knew that two members of the local Party committee shared my opinion, and I told them that honesty required them to speak up. This annoyed them so much that they were glad to see the back of me. I had married in the meantime, however, and the main reason for my departure was that my wife didn't take to the climate in the Oderbruch.

I now went to Greifswald and, together with a single secretary, revived the university newspaper from scratch. It was a nice little paper, printed in two colours, and was well received by the Party. When I had been working on *The Line* in Seelow, I had written an article strongly attacking one of the farmers, a Communist, who refused to join the collective farm. Fortunately, one of the old Party hands—a type that is now less and less common—drummed it into my head that this wasn't the way to treat a comrade. This invaluable experience made me less dogmatic in my attitudes, so that I was able to get on good terms even with non-Party staff members on whom the rigid Party secretary had been unable to make much impression. He was a pleasant sort of man from a working-class background, fortunately aware of his limitations, but he was soon replaced by a less self-confident man who seemed to have formerly been in a higher post. The University itself didn't come under the local Party branch but was directly controlled by the Science Division of the Central Committee.

The new Party secretary couldn't make much headway with the University staff either—he was too inflexible, a man who carried out orders, whereas I had the feeling that people preferred officials like me. My view at the time was that we had to take the Party as it was and appreciate its history and mode of functioning; but that once I and like-minded Party members took charge—which could not be far off—we would be able to carry the people with us.

Tell us a little more about the paper you edited.

It came out every two weeks and was simply called *Our University*: 'Journal of the Socialist Unity Party in the Ernst Moritz Arndt University of Greifswald'. I found a printer, collected information from contacts in all the faculties, and made a really nice job of it. Greifswald was an old university, founded in the fifteenth century, but it had always been small and only had three faculties: Philosophy, Medicine and Natural Sciences. There were no more than two-and-a-half or three thousand students. Ideal!

Two events stand out during this period: the death in 1960 of Wilhelm Pieck, who greatly attracted me, though I never actually met him; and the building of the Wall on 13 August 1961.

I was all in favour of the Wall. Except in Berlin perhaps, comrades like myself thought that the sealing of the frontier would allow us to concentrate on winning people's support, rather than snooping on them with the suspicion that they intended to leave for the West. The 13th of August came in the middle of my time in Greifswald, when things were not working very well between my wife, Gundula, and myself. She didn't like the place and had been made to do an unpleasant job for the German-Soviet Friendship Society—a stillborn organization which has done a few useful things over the years. Still, although she also had a miscarriage during the period, I can safely say that they were two of the happiest years in my life.

Did the 13th of August come as a complete surprise, or were people prepared for it?

The date itself was a complete surprise. It was rather like the coming of Christ—people didn't believe it would happen, but it did. Something had to be done to stop people escaping to the West. I didn't myself think that something so drastic and semi-military as a wall would be put up, but once it was there, I completely approved of it.

Did you have any ideological arguments about the Wall with people at Greifswald University?

Except for some problems in and around Berlin, the building of the Wall was a complete success from the ideological point of view as well.

But surely there was some grumbling among the population?

Of course, but it was mostly quite subdued. The important thing to realize is that to be in what was once part of Hitler's Germany is very different from being in any other Eastern bloc country—not excluding Hungary, which had the Horthy regime. The Soviet-style councils set up in Germany after the First World War were destroyed and the working-class movement was defeated—that is a historical responsibility we have to bear. In time, when the younger generations that have had nothing to do with Nazism come to maturity, the GDR may well grow more like other East European countries, but in 1961 memories of the past were still so strong, with the Russian presence as a constant reminder of Germany's defeat, that the Wall generally corresponded to the will of the population. People just accepted the official interpretation, as part of what I call the Hermann Kant syndrome. Since resistance was pointless, all one could do was grumble.

The only real possibility was the emergence of a Dubček-type group, with ideas of liberalization; or—an unpleasant alternative—a worsening of the economic situation to the point that the younger generation rose in protest. If what has been happening recently in Poland were to happen in the GDR, heaven knows what the result would be. One can only hope that things remain stable, in the GDR as in Moscow. It is in everyone's interests that the Western supporters of detente should continue to follow the Brandt-Bahr line and try to take the pressure off the GDR. For if the state is forced to defend itself, attitudes will harden and stricter laws will be introduced, as they were at Easter 1979.

How did you view the Ulbricht leadership during that two-year period?

After Ulbricht and his people had established their authority in 1958, there followed a strange mixture of a little liberalization and a little of the Chinese Cultural Revolution. It was all very much in the Ulbricht style, but the sort of thing that satisfied people like myself. The Party was content with my work, and although—or, rather, because—I was always discussing different things from my colleagues, I was sent to the Berlin Headquarters of the Trade Union for Scientists and University Staff, with the job of introducing some flexibility into its rigid, inefficient bureaucracy. A few other younger people came from the Philosophy Department to give fresh blood to the organization. It was a time when I was still in harmony with the Party line, with myself, and with the comrades from the Science Department of the Central Committee.

What was the nature of the trade union you went to work for? More generally, how would you describe the difference between trade unions in Western and Eastern Europe?

It embraced all those who worked in universities, technical colleges and the Academy of Science, from professors down to cleaning women. Only the students were expected to join a separate organization: the FDJ.

The Union's job was, on the one hand, to protect its members against bureaucratic tendencies at their place of work—though it didn't do much in that field—and on the other hand to train people in the modes of socialist administration and the like. In practice this meant that, as in every publicly owned industry and factory, the Union had to involve everybody in drawing up a plan of work and to ensure that it was carried out. There was also discussion of welfare measures and improvements in working conditions, but the main business was to plan the work of the relevant unit. The slogan ran: 'Share in the work, share in the planning, share in the decision-making.' Alongside the ideological strengthening of the union through meetings and special colloquia, we organized discussion on the educational programme, university administration, the implementation of Party directives, and so on. Maybe the difference between this and a normal trade union in the West is not all that great.

Although trade unions in socialist countries have no real say on wages and salaries, they do exercise certain welfare functions, such as allocating holiday accommodation or places in kindergartens. They also play a role in settling workplace disputes. In fact people at the top very rarely win their case in the labour court when they try to dismiss someone, because it is always possible to prove that they themselves have neglected their duty in one way or another. No one gets the sack just for pissing against the wall, to put it vulgarly.

I had the impression that union activity is more profitable at university level than it often is in industry. We managed to give a platform for at least some of the younger lecturers to air their views on the rather ossified features of university life, and the Party leadership attached considerable importance to direct links with us. Kurt Hager, for instance, came and listened to our ideas. However, I must have spoken my mind a little too freely, because I was transferred to an advisory post dealing with everyday union business such as the preparation of the chairman's visit to a provincial town.

It was during my time with the union that I finally lost my political naïveté. The most important thing I learnt was that the Party really consists of two parties, the same as the two that emerged in Czechoslovakia in 1967–68. One sticks to the status quo, adopting a basically authoritarian position; while the other favours deep reforms, seeking out discussion and giving rational answers to awkward questions. I was convinced that the second of these would eventually win through, but my residual Party solidarity and my belief in open debate still held me back from seeing the necessary struggle in fully antagonistic terms. Another milestone for me had been the 15th anniversary celebrations of the GDR in 1964, when I became aware that I wasn't happy with the way things were going. The tone of the anniversary was just one of self-congratulation for past achievements, with no conception of the future. This proved that the revolution was over as far as the GDR was concerned, and that we were expected to be happy with what we had. That contradicted everything I believed in. I remembered studying Hegel at university, and what was happening in the GDR seemed to me like a reproduction of Hegel's attitude towards the state. It was not that I actually sought a confrontation: I still did not realize what an impediment the Party apparatus was to the progress of socialism. But I wanted to see things continue to develop, and it was clear by then that the hopes one had pinned on the closing of the frontiers in

1961 had not been fulfilled. When I left the union in 1965, I joined the intellectual journal *Forum*, whose editor supported the liberal tendencies that had made themselves felt since 1958 and were very soon to be quashed. I had already written once or twice for *Forum* and the new job marked my complete change of direction. Since 1964 I had taken the line of Mao and accepted his criticisms of Khruschev and the Soviet Union. At the same time I was highly indignant at the way Khruschev had been dismissed—though only later did I learn about the army's role in the affair.

At *Forum* I took a kind of radical left-wing position, with as much basic Marx as possible—Maoism was out of the question. On one occasion I wrote an article criticizing the writer Günter Kunert from a left-wing position, as a result of which he was refused permission to go abroad. Although the matter was eventually patched up, people said that the line I had taken made me look like an agent provocateur. My view, however, was simply that *Forum* should be *the* journal for students and young intellectuals. A new editor then arrived from Moscow—I was assistant editor—who showed me his doctoral dissertation in which he had written that if Stalin were to return, he should be opposed right from the start. This gave me a certain hold over him, whenever he lacked the moral strength to carry his opinions through or became ill with worry over an article of his that went further than it should have done. He was a thoroughly decent man who found himself in a very difficult position. But in the end he was glad when I left. I told him that all we were doing was throwing sand in people's eyes, and that I couldn't stand it any longer.

All this time, my situation had become more and more delicate. The last straw, as far as the Party was concerned, was an article I wrote against the excessive conformism and lack of criticism in policy matters. The Party tried to get experts to condemn what I had written, but although they said my arguments were not always correct, they saw no reason to take the matter further. Then came the 11th Plenum of the Central Committee, with which I completely disagreed.

What happened at the Plenum?

It was the meeting that suddenly halted the more liberal cultural policies pursued since 1956. I didn't necessarily agree with the views of people like Volker Braun and his portrayal of the working class in the play *Kipper Paul Bauch*, but I did not conceal my opinion that such things ought to be discussed openly, not swept under the carpet.

I was popular among all my colleagues in general, but the Central Committee couldn't accept what I was doing, and I imagine that words were exchanged behind the scenes, to the effect that Comrade Bahro couldn't possibly be allowed to stay in his present position. They wanted to keep me quiet, so for nine months I was just given the job of reviewing a couple of periodicals—something I could do at home, together with a lot of other reading. This was between autumn 1966 and May 1967. One of the things I read at this time, I think, was Trotsky's autobiography.

How did you manage to get hold of it?

Books from the West continually found their way across. The Swiss Communist I mentioned earlier, for example, used to bring things in from West Berlin. I had reached the point at which I had to work out where I really stood, and what 'actually existing socialism' represented. I knew it was very different from what Marx and Engels had envisaged, and my study of Deutscher's book on Stalin confirmed my view that objective forces, not subjective acts of sabotage, were the basic cause. Having read Marx's *Grundrisse*, I began a discussion with the medieval historian Siegfried Wolgarst, who put me on to Karl Wittvogel. Deutscher, Wittvogel's *Oriental Despotism*, Gramsci—these were the influences that set my mind working along the lines followed in my book. But I wasn't yet set on a collision course. The final stage came only in 1968, after the events in Czechoslovakia.

This was the period, 1966–67, of the cultural revolution in China. To what extent did this influence you? And how does Trotsky fit in?

Whether one calls it Maoism, Trotskyism or some other name, the initial attitude is that the revolution has been betrayed. Everybody goes through this stage. But I have moved further and further from such terminology and eventually arrived at my present position—that of Eurocommunism.

As to the Chinese Cultural Revolution, I only really learned about it later, in 1969–70 or perhaps even 1971. There was a book on it by Giovanni Bluma that I found especially important.

In an article I wrote in 1967 or thereabouts, I argued that the 'brake' on economic and political revolution lay in the Party apparatus itself. In December 1967 I wrote a letter to Ulbricht drawing attention to the new action programme in Czechoslovakia, as well as to the significance of developments in Yugoslavia. From 1968 onwards I read the Belgrade journal *International Politics* every month.

Did you get this privately?

No. I ordered it officially through the press office, in spite of the risks involved after the intervention in Czechoslovakia.

Were you able to receive Chinese literature in the same way?

No—there wasn't much to be had. I used to go to the Chinese Embassy to look at what was displayed outside, but there was only information about the harvest and other economic matters. I did have the four-volume selection of Mao Tse-tung's works, and I understood his argument that since there were no class forces in China ready to ward off the process of bureaucratization, young people had to be mobilized to prevent a repetition of Stalin. But I also realized what a failure that attempt had been.

Did you not find it a problem that Mao's thinking was apparently so similar to Stalin's?

The affinities between Mao and Stalin didn't strike me as fundamental, because I thought that Mao could steer a political course that bypassed Stalinism.

Letters were exchanged at this time between the Soviet Communist Party and the Chinese government. Were you able to read the text of the Chinese letters?

The early ones, from 1964, were published in *Neues Deutschland*, but afterwards only the Russian letters appeared. Still, all the basic arguments were presented in 1964, and I always kept a copy of such things.

To what extent were the differences between the Soviet Union and China discussed in the base organizations of the SED?

I can't give you a precise answer because I was caught up in the Party apparatus at the time. I know that they were discussed, but in general it was intellectuals not workers who read the long articles in *Neues Deutschland*. After the withdrawal of Soviet advisers from China, it became obvious to everyone that it was not just an ideological conflict. But although there was some discussion at university trade-union meetings, the purpose of Party meetings was, as always, to lay down the official line. The actual split certainly had an unsettling effect, so that people began to wonder whether there might be several kinds of Marxism and not just a single universal gospel. But I doubt that the majority gave it much thought. It was not the sort of thing one discussed openly, and we were given only the information they thought we needed.

What proportion of Party members are, in fact, concerned with ideological questions? Is it a small minority?

We are basically talking about the ideological sector of the apparatus, including people working at the Central Committee's Institute of Social Sciences, the Marxism-Leninism Institute, and university departments ranging from German and History to the more explicitly ideological subjects. There are also a number of non-Party people interested in Marxist thought, most of them sophisticated thinkers well versed in the Western literature. But as far as the Party as a whole is concerned, you will hardly find a single member in an average factory or office who gives a moment's thought to such questions. At the most, some may have been passively aware that Russia and China were at loggerheads, or even have regretted in discussion that the two great socialist countries should, to the benefit of the capitalist world, be working against instead of with each other. The local Party secretary would naturally know about it as well, because he would have been told the line at his monthly briefing. If critical views are expressed at meetings, the Party secretary is expected to report them to the district committee. But if he reports, say, seven such criticisms and the secretary in the next factory only reports three, then a bad mark is chalked up against him, so he thinks twice before saying anything.

Similarly, people on the shop floor don't tell the Party secretary everything that is said. Suppose there's a proposal for a price increase. The shop-floor representative wouldn't tell the Party secretary that the workers were highly critical of it, but only that a few of the men didn't fully understand the position and still had a few queries. In this way, differences of opinion rarely make themselves heard.

But was there any kind of unofficial pro-Chinese feeling among members of the Party?

To some extent, yes. It started with the establishment of the People's Communes and lasted until the end of the Cultural Revolution—though in the GDR we learnt about these things comparatively late. It came to an end when we realized that what was happening was again limited to a small bureaucratic group and not shared by the whole population, as Mao had intended. It may be better, in any case, to call it an anti-Soviet attitude rather than a pro-Chinese one. What attracted us was the different, more democratic way of doing things—the wall newspapers, for instance, which involved the masses as an anti-bureaucratic force. Our information came, of course, from official Chinese sources.

What impact did these Chinese sources have on your discussions?

They were not a springboard for oppositional attitudes on our part, but rather served as a kind of analogy. Comrades, we would say, there is a real danger that the Party bureaucracy may separate itself from the masses, and Lenin said that it was the job of the unions to protect the masses against such developments; maybe what is happening in China runs parallel to this; and anyway we are entitled to be given more information about what is really happening in China. Then the Party secretary would reply that these were complicated matters, that we must beware of allowing the enemy to exploit the situation, that the Chinese communes had economic problems of their own and so on. Someone might even quote from the West German paper *Die Zeit*. But in such discussions there is never any direct confrontation with the official Party line—the most one gets is a formalized pattern of questions and answers.

Did the Party have private internal information about what was happening in China?

I never saw any, though I assume they must have had. I wasn't in an important enough position to see such material. But, as I said, all our discussions were limited to the Chinese developments themselves, with no hint that they might have some relevance for us too; whereas I, and others who thought like me, wanted to use them for a radical re-examination of basic Marxist principles.

It was the same with Trotsky. No one can read Trotsky, even if they argue with what he says, without realizing that he is right. People in the Institute for Marxism-Leninism, in Philosophy Departments at universities and other branches of the ideological Party apparatus are well aware of this, so that the anti-Trotsky articles they write only deal with marginal points, not with his basic position. The top members of the Party intelligentsia know perfectly well what the position is, but the majority of them still maintain that, for the sake of stability, the religion must be preserved intact and the dogma preached to the masses. A friend of mine once wrote a play about Lenin and Trotsky, and Kurt Hager, a member of the SED Central Committee, said to him personally: 'Comrade, you can't talk about such things before our Soviet comrades have done so.'

Does one ever hear the old story that Trotsky was a Nazi agent?

No, no, those days are over, although you might still find the odd lunatic prepared to believe such stuff. Most Party members just

don't know who Trotsky was, and the only people who know anything about his criticism of Comintern policy in Germany in the
1930s would be those specially assigned to deal with that period. The
SED's achievements in German labour history are written up in the
spirit of Stalin's made-to-order history of the CPSU, though not quite
so crudely. As a result, discussion of historical questions, and
especially of conflicts within the workers' movement, is virtually
blocked from the start.

*The official eight-volume history of the German working-class
movement states that, in the so-called third period, it was a mistake
to talk of social-fascism and not to preserve the unity of the working-
class movement. What is not said, however, is that whereas the KPD
refused to accept a united-front policy, there were men such as Trotsky who did support it.*

The point is that, although whoever wrote this chapter was well
aware of Trotsky's position, the various Party secretaries who might
read it are not interested in such historical analyses but are just looking for an account of how the period is officially assessed. You must
also remember that historical continuity has been lost in Germany,
first through the Nazis, then through the SED. The SED was founded
not as the result of ideological discussions but as a consequence of
the failure of Social Democracy in Germany, as a kind of settlement
of the historical account. A few intellectuals, like university professors, had their own problems to settle in this connection, but for
the mass of people in the Party—including myself, I must say—all
that is over and done with. Similarly, I see little relevance for today
in the conflict between the older and younger generation in the Social
Democratic movement of the 1880s. And the German working-class
movement collapsed so utterly in 1933 that there is no way of re-
establishing a continuity.

You said earlier that you read Lenin's State and Revolution *at
school. At one point Lenin argues that no official in the administration should earn more than a worker's wages. Were you not struck
by the contradiction between this and the reality in the GDR?*

First I should make it clear that I read it alone, at the urging of the teacher I told you about, who may have felt that I had it in me to exercise some influence in this direction in later life. Anyway, I was only fifteen or sixteen at the time, and I can't say that I was struck by this contradiction. In fact, lower-ranking administrative personnel were not paid all that much. When I was in Seelow in 1959, I got 700 marks per month gross, 500 marks net. In Greifswald I earned 800 or so, and in Berlin, in the trade union, 1,000 gross and 800 net. That was a little more than the average male worker's wage. Women got less, on average, because they did the less skilled jobs.

But didn't people realize that ministers and top Party officials are paid much more?

I don't remember that it was thought very important. The concept of the working man's wage is, of course, significant for those who know their Lenin, but it wasn't considered a vital issue. Much more central was the question of bribing intellectuals not to leave the GDR for the West. As to top salaries, these could be explained by the greater responsibilities and the pressure on the officials concerned.

The term 'actually existing socialism' (*realexistierender Sozialismus*) was coined to justify the contrast between what Marx and Lenin had said and what had actually developed. The advantages enjoyed by Party officials and Party members in the GDR are not really all that great, and they are also well concealed. For example, there is a special shop in the basement of SED headquarters in Berlin where rare items like bananas can usually be obtained, and there are also special hospitals and holiday hotels for Party officials. But I never came across any special shops in the provinces, and the average Party bureaucrat doesn't live much differently from his counterpart in a factory. The man at the top does not have the same perks as his opposite number in West Germany, simply because the GDR is a poorer country. It is true, however, that he would be provided with a Volvo or similar car, while the man in the street waits years and years for his little two-stroke Trabant.

Are such things criticized at Party meetings?

There could be more criticism than there is, without fear of reprisals. At the time when the Palast der Republik—a sort of congress centre—was being built in Berlin, I stood up at a meeting and said it would be better to spend the money on new flats. The Chairman retorted that all countries built such showpieces—to which I replied: 'That's the whole point!' But nothing ever happened to me as a result.

What about that reservation where top bureaucrats live?

It's an enclosed area near Wandlitz, north of Berlin, with its own guards and barbed-wire fences. Special roads had to be built so that they could travel without disturbance to their office in the city centre. As in Moscow, all the intersections are kept open when their cars are on the road. The reason given is security. The only man who managed to live in his own apartment outside the Wandlitz ghetto was old Wilhelm Pieck. But he and Grotewohl were truly exceptional people, widely accepted by the masses, in a way that nobody has been since. Honecker was a more sympathetic figure than Ulbricht, although he has long since lost the little sympathy he had.

Let us return to 1967 and the time when you had left Forum *but were still drawing your salary from them.*

I took a nominal cut from 1,200 marks a month to 1,100 marks, which didn't matter much.

Were you still allowed to publish articles?

Of course not.

Not even anonymously?

No. It would have been too dangerous for my colleagues, and I wouldn't have done so without a guarantee from someone higher up. In a case like that you have to wait a year or two for the dust to settle before venturing into the open again; then you get another Party member to phone a paper and tell them that you have been working in a factory for the past two years, and that things have changed sufficiently for them to accept an article from you again. Things are rather inflexible, however, and you have to get official permission to publish on ideological matters.

Although my independent views made me unsuitable for internal GDR work, it was thought that they could be put to use by the anti-Western propaganda department of the Central Council of the National Front. The head of the department was very keen to employ me, but the other two present at my interview—both of them women—reported to the vice-president of the Council that I had started to talk about China and was too lacking in self-criticism. In fact, I was quite relieved when I heard that I had not been given the job. In 1968 the head himself was fired for referring to the events in Czechoslovakia as 'intervention' and 'invasion' instead of 'fraternal assistance'.

So, the last article you ever published in the GDR was in 1967, when you were still working for Forum. *Is that right?*

Yes. The only other thing to appear was a few excerpts from my doctoral dissertation, published in a scientific journal of the Technische Hochschule Leuna-Merseburg. After 1968 I didn't try to publish anything, because I didn't want to identify myself in any way with the regime.

What did you do after those six months at home were up?

I'm not sure how it happened, but I had had enough of those ideological arguments and wanted to get back to the grass roots. The idea that I should go into industry therefore suited me down to the ground. A few years earlier a number of so-called Offices for Industrial Rationalization—rather like firms of management consultants in the West—had been established to supervise the factories and the various industrial complexes. One such Office had been set up with a staff of ten or so in the Berlin suburb of Weissensee, and I was given a job in charge of sociological aspects. In other words, I had to apply certain psycho-sociological principles in the factories where rationalization was under way; to smoothe over, as it were, the psychological and sociological problems inevitably bound up with proposals for greater efficiency.

The manager of this Office, a graduate engineer from Riesa in Saxony, was suspicious of me because the Party had pushed me into the job over his head. But I got on well with the others after they discovered that I was the sort of person they could talk to, a person who wasn't prepared just to accept things as he found them. I had the same experience later when I was in jail in Bautzen.

I was able to do a good deal of useful work. Sometimes I could see what needed to be done in a factory more quickly than those on the spot, but there were always obstacles to be overcome. Once, I remember, it had been proposed to reconstruct an old building to take new machines, even though a new building in the vicinity was just being used as a warehouse. I pointed out that it would be more sensible to use the old place as a warehouse, and to instal the new machinery in the other building. But this put the whole planning process into question and since the manager ultimately had more power, I had to accept the situation and concentrate on specific matters of economic and technical organization.

Which industries were you involved with?

I started with rubber and asbestos: tyres and rubber components for cars, conveyor belts for the lignite mining industry, latex products like surgical rubber gloves, and a variety of asbestos products. Later I moved on to plastics, which included kitchen utensils, industrial containers, and so on. All this made up the so-called Rubber Plastics Kombinat. The whole industry employed some thirty thousand workers in factories scattered over the country. The Office headquarters were in Halle, and it was uneconomic to have our group working in Berlin. But since we wanted to stay there, they transferred us to the Berlin Rubber Works, a smaller organization with some three thousand employees. You always have to expect that someone will inform on you if you speak your mind in discussions. As far as I could tell, however, I wasn't considered important enough after the *Forum* episode. My colleagues also regarded me as naive—'Rudi's crazy', they would say. At the interrogation after my arrest, they mentioned a fellow-student who had reported that I once got drunk during a spell of work on the land and compared myself to Lenin. This proved I was crazy, he had said, but it also showed I could not possibly be a traitor to the cause. In the event his evidence probably weighed in my favour. A certain naîveté really is characteristic of me: people who do what I did are probably not quite normal.

In the Soviet Union you would probably have been put in a psychiatric clinic.

My interrogator also wondered, only half-jokingly, whether I was *compos mentis*. It reminds me of those despotic oriental regimes where anybody who goes against the official line is regarded as not quite normal.

How did you come to write the letter to Ulbricht in 1967 that you mentioned earlier? Was it the product of discussion with others?

I should make it clear that, although I did not stop discussing things, I followed my own ideas after 1968. In the letter, I started from the subaltern position of the working class in the GDR and proposed, not a return to the position from which Yugoslavia had developed its own form of socialism—which would have been unrealistic—but a kind of combination of centralized control and mass democracy. I addressed my letter to Ulbricht not as First Secretary of the Central Committee but as Chairman of the Council of State, because in the latter capacity he had an obligation to reply within eight weeks.

When eight weeks had elapsed without a reply, I wrote a second letter. Finally, in May 1968, a man from the economics department of the Central Committee turned up at my office to talk things over with me. He pointed out that since my proposals were already part of official policy, there must be some other reason behind my persistent criticism. We then talked about Czechoslovakia, and he asked me what I thought about Smrkovsky's declaration that the Czechs would defend themselves against an armoured push from the north. I answered that, provided no preparations were being made to intervene in Czechoslovakia, I didn't approve of what Smrkovsky had said. There was a genuine clash of ideas between us, and as long as the Czech situation remained unclear, people like me were not summarily dealt with.

How long did the discussion last?

About three hours. There was actually an amusing side to it. When he left, he said: 'Comrade, if you go on like this, there will be an unholy row with the Party.' But the day had started quite differently. When someone comes from the Central Committee, he doesn't go directly to the person he wants to see but first calls on his superior. That morning my boss was not yet there, and so we chatted for a while without his realizing that I was Rudi Bahro, or without my giving any hint that I had heretical views. When he left, he said he would never have guessed that I was the cause of all the trouble.

You said that much of the discussion was about Czechoslovakia. Did Party members have any access to information about the real situation?

No, there were only the *Neues Deutschland* reports. What really interested us were the things they did not mention.

Did you listen to West German radio?

It must have been when I was working for the trade union that I started to listen to Western broadcasts. But my first encounter was with Erich Fried's BBC programme for GDR listeners, especially his reports on the Italian, French and other European communist parties. When I was working for *Forum*, I came across West German material in the course of my duties.

Have you travelled much in Czechoslovakia and elsewhere in Eastern Europe?

No, I hardly travelled at all. In 1958, when I was still a loyal supporter of the Party line, I visited the Soviet Union as a member of an FDJ delegation, following publication of some of my poems. I also made a few trips to Czechoslovakia, but I did not go there at all in

1968. I knew much more about developments in the Soviet Union, Poland, Hungary and Czechoslovakia—not Romania or Bulgaria— than those who had actually been there, either because I knew Party members in these countries or because I had close contact with comrades in the GDR who had studied in the Soviet Union and had links with it. My wife from whom I was later divorced had read Slavonic Studies, and she helped me to get to know the history of Soviet literature in considerable detail. I was already familiar, of course, with the history of the Soviet Communist Party.

Do you know Russian?

Not enough to read it fluently. But over the years I have probably spent more time studying Russian than German history.

All in all then, you felt quite well informed at the time of the Prague Spring?

Yes. Although I had only been there a few times, I felt that I clearly understood what it was like to live in Czechoslovakia, and I experienced the events of 1968 as if I had been personally present. I would read *Neues Deutschland* thoroughly and then listen to Western radio stations. We only bought a television later, when the children were older. At the time of the Prague Spring, I somehow managed to get the German-language *Prager Zeitung* which printed the Action Programme of the Czechoslovak Communist Party. I also had two or three copies of *In the Heart of Europe*, a Czech review for overseas consumption. It was in one of these, in 1968, that Zdenek Mlynař published an article which had a decisive influence on my way of thinking.

In The Alternative *you make certain criticisms of the way the Prague Spring developed. Did you hold those views in 1968 itself?*

No. I only began to think in that way after I had read the Richter Report in 1972 or 1973. News of such things always takes some time to emerge in Eastern bloc countries, and I had no access to official sources of information.

In which Party base organization were you at the time?

First there was the Party organization in the plastics and rubber combine in Berlin. Later there was the group of just three of us who still belonged to the Halle-based enterprise and therefore had our own organization. I was secretary of this group and attended the monthly briefings for Party secretaries in the district.

This was in 1968?

No, no, that was 1974–5.

But in 1968 you were in favour of the Action Programme and the other developments in Czechoslovakia.

I identified completely with developments in Czechoslovakia, and the only time in my life when I've slept badly was after the news of the Russian invasion.

How did people in general react to the invasion? Did you discuss it in your Party organization?

At first there was absolutely no public discussion about Czechoslovakia. Because of the Soviet military presence in the GDR, the man in the street saw little possibility that anything similar would happen there. Those, like me, who were critical of the regime had far greater hopes, but the average citizen, despite some sympathy for what was happening, was sceptical about its prospects. In the weeks before the invasion, people began to hear of GDR troop movements near the Czech border and grew increasingly afraid that war would break out. On the day of the invasion, there was an atmosphere of apprehension in the trains and buses, as people talked about the danger of war and the part their own soldiers were playing. I sat down in a corner, wrote my letter of resignation from the Party, and then went to see a friend who was equally concerned about the situation. Without directly contradicting me, he implied that I ought not to resign from the Party. I prepared a statement and intended to announce my resignation after making it public. I telephoned the Czechoslovak Embassy on 23 or 24 August, gave my name and started to dictate my condemnation of the invasion. The man in the embassy interrupted me and said that the phone was probably being tapped. When I replied that that didn't worry me, he said that my action was pointless, that the invasion was a *fait accompli* and that they wouldn't publish my statement anyway. All that interested him was how old I was and whether I was a member of the Party. I thought things over. If my statement wasn't going to have any impact, there was no point in issuing it: better to work out in my own time the nature of the 'actually existing socialism' that had occupied my thoughts since my days at *Forum*. But although I didn't resign, I made my views clear enough at Party meetings.

How strong was the opposition to you at those Party meetings?

In such matters twenty or thirty per cent usually support you, at least in private, while a further thirty per cent or so are secretly sympathetic and like to hear people speaking up. It's only the members of the Party apparatus who actively oppose you.

What form did these discussions take? Were there arguments about Dubček and so on?

Yes. I always brought these things up. Then someone would put the counter-argument, without driving the matter to extremes. It would be said that the Czechoslovak Communist Party had made serious mistakes which we in the GDR would never have made; that the petty-bourgeois and other reactionary forces who posed such a danger in Czechoslovakia had mostly left the GDR and fled to the West; in other words, that we in the GDR had arranged things much better and didn't have such problems.

The Party knew exactly where I stood on the question, but no action was taken against me. There were a large number of Party members who thought as I did, I'm sure, and who were simply afraid to come out into the open when they looked at the general situation in the country and at the personal risks they would be running.

Do you think these matters were discussed in other Party organizations than your own?

I have good reason to believe that a number of those who took a similar position would not have done so without my lead.

How did you react to the other things that were happening in the world in 1968?

1968 was for me the most important of all years. I was very excited about the Tet Offensive in Vietnam, which came at the same time as the Dubček reforms. Then there were the May events in Paris, which showed me for the first time how progressive tendencies in East and West were linked. This is still basic to my ideas today.

What about events in West Germany?

I heard that there was a so-called New Left movement, but I didn't attach as much importance to it as to the French events. In fact, I was surprised by what happened in West Germany, for our discussions with West Germans and West Berliners between 1954 and 1959 had been totally unproductive. There was a direct confrontation, and I could see no difference between SPD and CDU supporters. As to Paris, I cherished a few illusions at the start, not realizing how dogmatically they interpreted their Marxism.

3
The Alternative and Prison

*Let us move on now to the writing of your book. When did the idea
first begin to develop in your mind?*

I had already wanted to write a dissertation on scientific policy when
I was working for the Union of Scientists and University Staff in
Berlin, but I did not have any time after I joined *Forum*. My period
at *Forum* spelt the end of my political innocence, and as deputy
editor I accepted articles that took a different stance from that of the
Party, though not with any intention of seeking a confrontation. Today a lot of Party members accept completely the analysis in the first
two parts of my book, yet maintain that the conclusion is utopian
and that I ought not to have published it as I did. Although I can see
their point, I should stress that I wasn't looking for a confrontation.
If it had been possible, I would have tried to form my own wing
within the Party.

It was essentially my own experiences that set me thinking along
the lines that eventually led to *The Alternative*. However, my reading
in the 1960s—Deutscher, Wittvogel, Gramsci—guided my resolve to
elucidate the social system of 'actually existing socialism'. I was also
influenced by an old-guard Communist, the son of a working-class
family from the Ruhr, who told me about the Chinese problem and
warned me against becoming a mindless 'revisionist'. He was opposed to my line of thinking, especially to the Eurocommunism which
my book supports, and when I last saw him, shortly before my arrest, he became furious and told me I was just encouraging the
bourgeoisie and would bring disaster on us all. This was probably
due in part to his experience in a Nazi concentration camp—he

hasn't moved with the times and can't always grasp the present situation.

As to Deutscher's *Stalin*, I regard this as the most important book for an understanding of the situation in Eastern Europe—more important even than Roy Medvedev. On the one hand he almost provides a justification for Stalin. On the other he subjects him to a fundamental criticism, so that one can study the problem from both angles. Intellectuals in the Soviet Communist Party need to know this book. Deutscher's *Unfinished Revolution* is equally important, and I remember hearing his talks on the radio. In the same way my own book is not just criticism but also a kind of indirect apologia for the Russian Revolution and the whole non-capitalist line of development. I consider it important to keep both sides of the question together.

In one essential respect, however, I depart from Deutscher's conception. I take account of the Asiatic tradition, whereas Deutscher maintains, like Trotsky, that the revolution was betrayed from within.

The third writer you mention is Gramsci. What did you know of his?

A book of selections, published in West Germany, which gave a good general survey. Years ago there was an idea of publishing a translation in the GDR, but it never came off. In a sense, both Wittvogel and Gramsci were more important for me than the Trotskyist perspective. My main sociological concern was the division of labour, and while Wittvogel treated it in the Oriental context, Gramsci examined the psychological relationship between politics and the rational processes of economics. Something that strikes me now as more important than it did then is that Gramsci undertook a reinterpretation of the history of the Church, which I find very relevant to the needs of today.

Did you read Marcuse?

No, but one often learns about ideas without reading the original sources. All I knew of the Frankfurt School was Adorno's writings on music. I hadn't read Benjamin, for instance, but his ideas came out in discussions on Eisler, as did those of the Frankfurt School as a whole.

Do you know Marcuse's early work on Soviet Marxism?

Yes. I read it in 1969, as it happened. I also read Iring Fetscher's *From Marx to the Soviet Ideology*, but it was too early for me to grasp its significance. Even if I had read Marcuse at that time, I doubt whether I could have done much with him, because such matters cannot be solved on an ideological level.

So one could say that the Frankfurt School had little influence on Party intellectuals?

It may have influenced a few who were working on aesthetics, the history of literature, and so on. Wolfgang Heise, for example, had a thorough knowledge of the Frankfurt School. A colleague lent me some Wilhelm Reich, who struck me as quite important though not in the category of Deutscher, Wittvogel and Gramsci.

The interesting thing about Marcuse is that your rejection of the leading role of the working class is also prominent in his work. But there was no influence?

No.

Did the name Althusser mean anything in the GDR?

I knew the name, but I have always regarded such textual discussions of Marx's work as a pointless scholastic exercise. After I had written the book, I got to know a number of other writers: Garaudy, for example, whose earlier writings are in the old Marxist mould. But, you know, even the worst Stalinists from Western Europe are regarded as subversive in Eastern Europe.

That's surely an exaggeration!

Not really. They argue much more flexibly and freely, forcing you to confront new facts and problems to the point that you sometimes lose sight of what they are arguing against.

Another good book is Garaudy's work on Hegel, *God is Dead*, which was quite important for my intellectual development. I would adopt Garaudy's methodology myself if I were to write about philosophers—the question of historicity and how one shapes the ideological tradition into which one is born. Then there was Teilhard de Chardin's *The Phenomenon of Man*.

You read it in translation?

Yes, it was published by the CDU's Union Verlag. It is a thoroughly materialist work, and I share its thesis that man has an ultimate goal and an ultimate purpose. Man cannot be reduced to the realities of a particular moment, for there are other, transcendental realities that form part of the historical process. What seems to me important is that Teilhard analyses the continuity of history in terms of human nature, even though he passes over the question of the underlying class struggle. These ideas were already in my head, but Teilhard's work played an important part in the final section of my book. I used to type out pages of the books that influenced me—Deutscher's *Stalin* or the Trotsky trilogy, for instance. Then, after I had written what I wanted to say, I would look back and take out the quotations I needed.

When exactly did you start to write your book?

My book is closely bound up with the question of my dissertation. It started with the events in Prague in August 1968, and was intended no longer as an immanent critique but as a frontal attack written in blunt language without reservations. It was a decision I took on 21 August itself, the day of the invasion. Hate is not part of my nature, but that was a day when I really felt hate.

Did you direct your hate at individuals or at the system? Or were they one and the same, as far as you were concerned?

I hadn't yet made a theory out of it, but it was obvious to me that the enemy was the whole Party apparatus, the politbureaucracies in the GDR and the Soviet Union.

How did the forces of the imperialist enemy fit into the picture?

Imperialism—the enemy without, so to speak—seemed to me to have nothing whatever to do with the situation in Czechoslovakia. The imperialists were simply there, as a fact of life. It reminds me of the situation with Luther and the Turks. The Church was against the Turks, and Luther was also against the Turks, but he said that we must first have our own Reformation in order to fight the Turks in a consequential manner.

As to the question of hatred, one only hates what one knows through close contact. Imperialism is an idea, an objectification, an external system that has to be destroyed. The first version of my book, in 1973, still had traces of this hatred, and I eradicated them in the course of my revision. One had to get over such emotions.

How did the writing of your first version proceed over the five years between 1968 and 1973?

For a year and a half or so after 1968 I did a great deal of preparatory reading—the Trotsky trilogy, Soviet writings on the question of peace and socialism, and so on.

Did you know Medvedev?

I only read *Let History Judge* after I had written the first version of my book. In any case, it limits itself to the late-Stalinist period and does not attempt a broad historical analysis.

I also had some correspondence with a man called Mikhail Livshitz. I knew him from my time at *Forum* when he had published a shortened form of my Beethoven essay in a Moscow philosophical journal. (This essay deals with the problem of how Beethoven, who was conditioned by a period of revolution, could preserve his creativity in the face of the ensuing reaction, overcoming the crisis of 1814–1817 to write his last quartets and piano sonatas and the Missa Solemnis.) I wrote to Livshitz that, after all that had happened, it was impossible simply to restore the Leninist tradition and the Leninist formulae. One advantage of my position was that, not being in an office or a factory, I could see things from the outside. In May 1970 I took a course on labour studies, and was given a month off to write an essay attacking the idea that Taylorism could be applied to scientists and technologists. The people at Merseburg Technical College thought highly of it and suggested I work it up into a proper dissertation in the philosophy department, where they were also interested in sociological questions. In this way, I obtained three months leave a year for three, or even four years, using most of this time to work on my more important project. Although I had to conceal this from my supervisor, of course, I still justify it on the grounds that I did submit my dissertation in the end. I probably started writing *The Alternative* in 1972 and finished it towards the end of 1973. If I had finished the first version at the time of the Berlin Youth Festival in the summer of that year, I would have used the opportunity to smuggle it out of the country. Then, once the first version was finished, I plunged into the dissertation and wrote it up between 1974 and 1975.

Some of the colleagues who read this early version of my book caused me to re-think aspects of the first two parts. But I have not yet encountered any criticism of the final section that has made me depart from my basic line of thought. This is also true of certain Czech Communists, now living abroad, who argue that East European countries can be cured with a dose of Western consumerism, rather than through a basic change in the political structure.

How many people read the first version of the book?

Fifteen.

The entire text?

Yes, and about half of them responded actively. The fact that they had got something out of it had a positive psychological effect and further strengthened my convictions. Nobody tried to discourage me, although one of them did tell me to put it out of sight in my drawer, not so much because of the effect it could have on me but because of the generally unpleasant consequences that would result.

These were Communist friends you had known well for a long time?

Yes, people I could trust. We never met all together but only two at a time—that was the way I communicated with them.

And it fully justified itself, since no one gave anything away?

Exactly. Only at the end, when the State Security knew something was up, did they set someone on my tail. I fell for it a few times, when someone approached me and said they wanted to hear my views.

So what happened after the first version of your book was finished?

I didn't publish it, for a number of reasons. First, I wasn't satisfied with it, but I couldn't work on a revision and complete my dissertation at the same time. Although nothing would have happened if I hadn't finished the dissertation, I had to avoid exposing myself to the criticism that I had spent all my time on something else at the expense of the working people. Then there were personal reasons, involving my young children. I divorced my wife Gundula in 1973, partly in order to ensure that my family would not suffer if the manuscript was discovered, but also because Gundula was not a rebel by nature and was afraid of the consequences. After the divorce I continued to live at home working on the book and sharing in the housework. We told the children too, though they couldn't fully understand, of course. Now I must tell you about the interviews that originally formed part of my dissertation.

I carried them out in 1973 and 1974 with graduates working in industry, in order to find out what was hampering their initiative and holding them back. I appended the interviews to my dissertation and handed them to my professor. He was somewhat shocked, and warned me to keep them safe, out of harm's way. He told me to leave them out of the dissertation, which didn't really need them, but I thought they were the best part of the whole project. Anyway, the Pro-Rektor of Merseburg Technical College saw a copy and confiscated it, labelling it 'Strictly Confidential'. Then he ordered me to hand over all the remaining copies and to tell him who knew about the matter. The interviews had been lying around in my office for six months or so, and my colleagues had helped me to put them together. I have always been rather naive in such matters.

The Pro-Rektor, who had been a ministry official for a long while before becoming an academic, said that my dissertation would obviously not be accepted. My supervisor defended it and stuck to his guns, partly because he liked me but also because it was the only course open to him. Two other professors, a sociologist and a social psychologist, wrote favourable reports on it, but the Pro-Rektor was probably under orders from the Party or the security people to reject it.

How did the security people get on to you?

I never really found out. The earliest evidence they produced was a telephone conversation of mine from 1975, but it is possible that the person at the other end of the line was already one of their plants.

Anyway, it was not until 1977 that my dissertation was finally rejected on the advice of two other experts they had called in. Meanwhile I had started to revise my book with the help of a fellow-Communist, especially the second part. I would have revised the first part too, but I had just read Dutschke and I realized that a discussion of his views would distract attention from my central line of argument. I revised the second part to take account of things I had learnt in my work on the dissertation, and the third part I virtually rewrote from scratch with the help of this colleague. I won't mention any names. Some of my colleagues were rather angry with me when the affair came out, and the political police never revealed all they knew. So I would like to keep the others out of it.

How long did the second version take?

From autumn 1975 to January 1977. When it was finished, I left Berlin with my friend Uschi—she came with me to the West—and hid myself in a little village, where I wrote the last two chapters on the economics of the cultural revolution.

But didn't you still have your job in the plastics combine?

Yes. But since I knew that the crunch would soon come, I took the whole of my annual holiday in January 1977 in order to complete the book.

Why were the interviews so much more 'dangerous' than the dissertation itself?

The people I talked to were quite open about what was wrong. Almost all were loyal citizens, many of them Party members, but what they said about their own position showed up the contradiction between the creative intellectual forces in the GDR and the conditions under which they were compelled to operate. In a sense, I suppose, it really was confidential material, and by not giving it to the authorities I broke the law for the first and only time. If there are no aggravating circumstances, this sort of thing is punished with up to two years in jail. In my case, however, they couldn't accuse me of disseminating information before it had been declared confidential but only of leaving it lying around afterwards. Although this wasn't a serious offence in itself, the fact that the material could have been exploited by anti-socialist elements provided an element of guilt on my part. There was nothing in it that endangered national security, but it contained a degree of detail which, they afterwards claimed, the other side could not possibly have known.

But did it not all refer to matters of economic and social organization?

Yes. The interviews dealt with how things actually worked in the factories and so on. If I had passed them to the West along with the dissertation, it would have been regarded as a serious divulgence of confidential information, carrying a maximum sentence of eight years. In fact, my interrogator was well aware that this had not happened. They could have incriminated me by leaking one of the interviews to the West, but I did not think they would risk it.

In 1975, before my dissertation was finished, they sent a man to see me who was obviously an informer. He had also written a doctoral dissertation, and I could have found him interesting if his personality had not been totally different from mine. It would seem that they had not done their homework properly: he fairly reeked of authoritarian attitudes, a nationalist, pro-German background, a marginal connection with the National Committee for a Free Germany. He was a music journalist by profession, the sort of man who would agree with a conductor that the plain, unvarnished truth might make his orchestra less willing to cooperate. Much as I begrudged the time, I thought it better to keep in touch with him. For if I had shown that I saw through him, they would probably have sent another, less obvious informer, who might have been more successful in getting me to admit the logical consequences of my position. But this was not the only thing that went wrong.

One of the fifteen copies of my book was in the hands of a weak sort of fellow who became afraid and gave it to a woman-friend. This woman found it too good to destroy and passed it on to a third person, who then passed it on to a fourth, who thought he had better inform the Philosophy Department at which I had been a student. This copy still had things in it that I had asked the original owner to erase. But although this was done on all the other copies, he had not done so on his own. This happened in October 1976, so they must have known about the business by then at the latest. There was another such case. A woman who was probably being blackmailed came to see me with an introduction from a close personal source. She was perhaps the person who most gained my confidence, and when I met her again, I told her that a copy of the first version of the book was already in the West and that arrangements had been made for the final version as well. She obviously passed this information on, reporting at the same time that I expected to get two years after a big hue-and-cry over the issue. I thought of writing to Kurt Hager, but then I remembered my experience with the letter to Ulbricht and realized it would be pointless. Besides, I wanted to force them to react to the book. In the end I even had time to read the proofs.

How did you find a publisher for the book?

I had no contacts in the West, and all that side of things was arranged by a highly respected SED member through a third party.

Although he didn't agree with my views, he thought that the book should be published and contacted the Europäische Verlagsanstalt. When I heard that the director was a Czech emigré, I was very keen on the idea. I also wanted *Der Spiegel* to feature it beforehand. The State Security let me get on with it—undoubtedly with the consent of Hager and the state apparatus. At some point they must have realized that it would raise a stir, and yet they decided to let things take their course. During my interrogation I told them directly that they needed a 'test case' to show Moscow the sort of thing with which they had to contend. When they learned about the *Spiegel* aspect, they probably suspected that Western intelligence was mixed up in it as well—which is why they initially arrested me under paragraph 100 on a charge of having links with enemy organizations. I am still not sure how much they actually knew: they may have thought that the West was about to launch a propaganda drive, with my book as a focal point. But my only links with the West were through long-standing Communists, German and others. Later a *Spiegel* correspondent brought me the proofs and took them back with him, together with the interview he did with me. But it was a fellow-Communist who took the manuscript over in the first place. This much I am prepared to say, without mentioning names.

And all this time you still had your job in the combine?

Yes. I went on working there right down to the day I was arrested.

Even after you had given two West German television interviews?

Yes. The GDR authorities deliberately allowed me to give them.

Deliberately?

Yes, of course, because by then they were following all my movements. They had photos of me on my way to the interviews and back to my house. And just before, I had visited that woman informer.

But it wasn't illegal for you to give the interviews.

No, not at that time, although it would be now. It would also be illegal for Western journalists to do such interviews now. My interview came out in the *Spiegel* of 22 August 1977. On the same day, as it happened, there was a Party meeting in the works. One of my comrades came up to me and said he had heard that a West Berlin radio station was going to broadcast an interview with me that evening. I don't know to what extent he shared my views, but I was on good terms with him, as I was with all my colleagues. I told him to keep it to himself for the moment.

An endless, boring discussion went on at the meeting, until finally I stood up and said I wanted to make a personal statement. There were only about fifteen or twenty members there, since many were on their August holidays. I said something like this: 'Comrades, nine years ago, in 1968, I changed my views. I never agreed with the invasion of Czechoslovakia, and since then I have written a book criticizing "actually existing socialism". All that has been made public today in an interview in *Der Spiegel*.'

At first there was silence...

You said it just like that?

Just like that.

And nobody interrupted you?

No, nobody. Then it started. 'You're a plucky chap, Rudi!' someone called out. Others asked me some questions, in a friendly tone. Then the Party secretary, with whom I had often discussed things in a pretty radical way, said: 'We all know you, Rudi, and we know what you think. But how could you talk to the *Spiegel*?' I was still personally popular with most of the people there, even when two days later they unanimously voted to expel me. The discussion petered out soon afterwards. I went home and listened to Beethoven quartets with Uschi.

The next day I went to work as usual. But my telephone hardly rang. My only calls were personal ones from people to whom it had not occurred that the phone would be tapped. The woman informer and another person who was obviously part of the same set-up rang to find out how I was reacting to the affair. I knew what to expect, and I behaved quite naturally and calmly. So the day passed rather uneventfully, though rumours must have reached almost everybody.

Did many listen to the broadcast?

I'm sure they did.

But none of them discussed it with you.

No. I went to my office again the following day. It was in a separate little building, and I had often typed there till late in the evening in breach of the regulations. But they all knew and trusted me. I left at the usual time and went home. About six o'clock, as I was having supper, the bell rang three times—not the way people usually ring. I opened the door. Three men were standing there, two of them the unpleasant types one expects to see on such occasions. They said there was a charge against me and that I was to go with them. I asked whether I should take anything with me, and they said no. They merely told me to unplug the refrigerator and other electrical appliances. Then, without laying hands on me at all, they told me to get into the car with them. On the way to the prison at Hohenschön-hausen, a northern suburb of Berlin, they advised me to behave quietly. When we arrived, they led me down one long corridor of cells after another, probably to show me what was in store. I was psychologically well prepared, but I had never tried to imagine what the prison would actually look like. It is a modern building dating from the 1950s or 1960s—a far cry from the Lublyanka.

They took me to the interrogation room, where two very different men were sitting, 'normal' comrades like the rest of us. One was about my age, while the other interrogator was a little younger. They smiled at me, brought me something to eat and drink, then asked if I was not afraid that it might be poisoned. But when I replied that they should not think me that simple, they must have realized I was not afraid of them. I even told them it was important for people not to be afraid of those in power, not to cast a shroud of mystery over the workings of authority.

Then they asked me how I would have reacted if the authorities had taken no action. I said that I would probably have re-examined my analysis of the situation, in case it was faulty. At this they smiled and said everything was fine. They asked me a few more questions and soon betrayed the name of the woman they had planted on me. I had given her a false publisher's name for my book, because I had still been slightly suspicious of her, and when they repeated this name I knew how the information had reached them. In general, however, they were still only trying to find out what sort of person I was, and they could see that I had anticipated the situation and was not afraid.

Had you been officially arrested at this point?

No. That only happened the next day, after I had spent the night in one of the cells. There was only one other man in it, and in fact it would have been overcrowded if all four beds had been occupied. This man was obviously not there by accident, yet I was taken in by him, as I usually am. I was also wrong to think that I had nothing to hide, for I had no idea of the importance they would attach to various details in determining the length of my sentence.

What happened the next day?

They told me I was being arrested under paragraph 100 of the Criminal Code on the grounds of associating with organizations hostile to the state. I found out that they knew about many things: for example, the seventy copies of the book that Uschi and another friend had helped me to photocopy and secretly distribute in the GDR. I had sent them out to friends of mine on the Monday that the interview was published in *Der Spiegel*. By telling me that they knew all about that, they tried to get me to say more. When it was obvious that they knew something, I would usually confirm it. And although I was probably tricked a few times, I generally told them no more than they already knew.

They started from the edges, so to speak, and worked inwards, trying to discover how the whole thing had originated, who had copies of my dissertation and interviews, who had arranged my contacts with the West, and so on. Their first aim was to find out as much as they could, whether or not they eventually decided to put me on trial. They had released Jürgen Fuchs, for example, after a series of interrogations, whereas Harich had been put in prison.

This was the second or third day, I suppose.

I suppose so, but I don't remember exactly. Then they started to threaten me...

Did you have the right to a lawyer?

No, not at this time. Weeks later, I had the assistance of Dr Klaus Gysi, son of the former GDR Minister of Culture, whom my ex-wife Gundula had helped to find. He didn't share my views, but he took advantage of all the legal possibilities to defend me, and I was entirely satisfied with the way he acted.

But does one not have the right to a lawyer during interrogation?

No. I was allowed to speak to Dr Gysi a few times while I was awaiting trial, always in the presence of my interrogator, but we were only allowed to talk about my affairs outside. During the whole time leading up to the trial I was cut off from the outside world. I put in a request to see Uschi, but even that was refused. They let me write her letters, then told me to write them again because I had said too much. So I soon lost contact with her and with everybody. Later they made out that she too, together with another friend of mine who had helped with the distribution of the copies of my book, had been arrested, and this affected the way I reacted—I'll come back to this in a moment. For six months I wasn't even allowed to read *Neues Deutschland*—the only things available in the prison library were German, French and English classic novels and a few reference books. Still, I used it to widen my knowledge: Stendhal's *Charterhouse of Parma* and *Scarlet and Black*, Romain Rolland's *Jean Christophe*, Bettina von Arnim, an anthology of *Sturm and Drang* literature, the memoirs of Bertha von Suttner and Malwida von Meysenbug, some historical novels, and so on. I was allowed to have up to five or six books in the cell at a time, and if the warder pushed one through the door that I had already read or that didn't interest me, I could give it back in return for another. Travel books I read too—I have always been interested in anthropology. One that I particularly remember was about the Easter Islands.

On one occasion, they set a trap by showing me a way to smuggle messages out of the prison. When I fell for it, they put me in solitary confinement and didn't even allow me to read books for five whole weeks. The cell I shared with the other man, incidentally, had two glass-tile windows facing east, though one couldn't see out, and there was a supply of warm water. The air was good and conditions were hygienic. The food, which was pushed through a hatch in the door, reminded me of a bad works canteen. But I could live on it and, except for the five weeks in solitary, I was able to buy things to the value of thirty marks. I was finally allowed to see Gundula in the February after my arrest, shortly after the first meeting with my lawyer.

Was it legal for them to keep you so long without visitors?

One reason was that I first said I wanted Uschi to visit me, and they used this to delay things.

In general, I must say, conditions were not too bad. There were different categories of food, for example, but they treated me as a standard prisoner throughout. By denying me reading matter for a while they were trying, of course, to get me to give away more information, but it was all done within the framework of the law. There was also a chessboard in the cell, although my cell-mate was not much good.

Did you always share a cell?

Yes, and always with the same man.

Was he also a political prisoner?

'Political' is a wide-ranging word. He had been a works director until he was convicted of doing some underhand trade deal with a friend in West Germany which, they claimed, had undermined the economy of the GDR. Having completed his six years, he was now being held for further interrogation, although that may have been a cock-and-bull story. He told me he had also been in a cell with Nitsche, the civil rights man who later raised a stir in West Germany.

It soon became apparent to me thay they knew all about the contact who had taken my dissertation to West Berlin, and that someone at vsA-Verlag must have been feeding them information. Only in this way could they have known so many details about the papers I had given him along with the dissertation. He had twice been warned when he came back from West Berlin that they had their eye on him and knew he was working with me—in fact, they made it clear that they knew all those who had been helping me. If they were going to charge me with anti-state activity, they would have to charge him in the same way. And if I didn't tell them what they wanted to know, they would pounce on my friends, search their houses and so on. They claimed they didn't want to make such a fuss, and proposed a deal whereby, if I talked, nobody else would be arrested, and those already under arrest would be released. You can hardly expect, they said, to be released as though nothing has happened, so if you give us some information, perhaps we can call the whole thing off. They kept quoting from cheap articles about me in West German papers— 'Nothing New in Bahro' and the like. But I didn't give an inch, because I was convinced I was right. That was the only point at which my interrogator lost his temper. He said that my obstinacy was enough for three interrogations.

What rank did your interrogator have?

He didn't tell me, though it was usual to do so. He wore civilian clothes, like all the others. He was intellectually my equal, not physically violent but with a cruel psychological streak. On one occasion he told me to re-write one of my letters, although it was obvious it wouldn't be passed anyway.

Was he in a position to discuss the contents of your book?

Certainly. We got on well with each other, and our discussions were highly satisfactory as far as the subject of my book was concerned. He went so far as to say that my views might well have a contribution to make to the way things developed in the long term. I always emphasized, as I stated in my application to renounce GDR citizenship, that I had worked actively for twenty years for the establishment of socialism in the GDR, and that my book was a contribution towards the further development of the country. When I said this to the interrogator, he replied that I shouldn't think the Party didn't know there were problems, but that was not the point under discussion.

Had he already read the book from beginning to end?

Yes, from beginning to end—and understood it as well. He had also read the dissertation.

Could you judge how well he knew his Marx?

He was a lawyer by profession, and was certainly acquainted with the Marxist theory of the state. To what extent he knew *Capital*, I can't tell.

Did he tell you anything about his career or personal life?

Nothing personal—he would have been careful not to do that—but I did get a feeling of the man's mind, and he taught me a few things. Take the man who was in the cell with me. He was there with good cause, because there is a problem of corruption in the GDR where trade deals with the West are concerned. There are many people in jail for good reasons, though sometimes the interrogation rides rough-shod over their rights. But I have come to accept that if the superpowers have their secret police, the GDR must too. The situation has to be seen as a whole. In the end my interrogator fell back on commonplaces about the class struggle and so on, but he knew they were commonplaces, and I had the impression that, unscrupulous as he was in his job, he had to wrestle with a certain number of problems. Perhaps he was too intelligent. Once, I said to him, 'You must give up this job if you want to save your soul!'

How did he respond to that?

He just clammed up. This was the time, in mid-November 1977, when they were saying that if I agreed to compromise, I could enjoy a sort of semi-legal status in the GDR. I replied that if I could continue having contact with those still prepared to risk it, and if a kind of indirect cooperation could be arranged with the Party, and provided all the other conditions were kept—such as an end to arrests and the ransacking of people's homes—then a compromise might be possible. He accepted all this, and they did in fact put an end to the arrests and so on. For my part, I then told him how the business had been arranged. I told no lies, because that would have harmed my cause, and I wanted to stay in the GDR until my trial. They actually asked me whether I wanted to go to the West as quickly as possible, but I replied that I wasn't going to let anyone steal the show, and that I wasn't interested in going to the West in any case.

So now I was forced to give details. I was in an awkward position, since the man who took my book over to West Berlin was one of three they could lay their hands on. They didn't know for certain who he was, but once I had agreed to the compromise, I had to tell the whole story. It worried me, and it still does to some extent, although they didn't want to take any action against him in any case. If I had cooked up some story, my team of interrogators...

Team of interrogators?

Yes. Although only one of them actually conducted the questioning, he consulted with a number of others. By this time they knew me and my friends so well that they could be sure that if I had shown someone my dissertation, I would have shown him the book as well. And it was obvious that, even though I could make out that some only knew bits of it, the man who took over the manuscript must have been acquainted with the whole work. At one stage, I think, they toyed with the idea of giving up the trial altogether, but that didn't work out.

Did they appeal to your loyalty as a Communist?

Not at that point. My interrogator was too subtle for that. He knew that we were enemies in the context of 'actually existing socialism', but he was still prepared to offer me a compromise.

How long did each interrogation last?

The normal period. They would always start between eight and nine, with at least an hour for lunch and an afternoon session from two to five.

How long were you in custody before the trial?

Almost ten months.

Is there any limit to the time one can be held in custody?

Strictly speaking, three months, but it can be automatically renewed.

When did they revise the charge against you?

In January, or perhaps as early as December, I was told that the charge of having links with anti-state organizations had been altered to the more serious one of espionage and betrayal of state secrets. They made it clear that they could blow up the charge just as they liked and would always find some way of proving it.

Did you get the impression that the chief interrogator was in close touch with people higher up?

Yes. Down to the point where he offered me a compromise, he had followed an entirely logical course. His offer was clearly the result of a decision taken elsewhere.

Do you think there was a file on you in the Politbureau?

The Politbureau probably discussed my case, but any file would have been kept by the secretariat. At the beginning they were utterly misinformed and thought there were others at work behind me. It took them quite a long time to realize I was acting on my own. Some two months before the trial, while I was writing my basic statement about the book, the head of the State Security interrogation department came and argued with me for two hours or so in Stalinist terms. He was a general of fifty or sixty, very smooth and relaxed about the whole business. But he saw everything in black-and-white terms and was convinced I was a tool of the imperialists.

He asked whether I was prepared to return to the Marxist-Leninist fold. And when I said no, he accused me of telling lies and tried to get me to admit that I was working for the imperialists and that it was very wrong of me to have recourse to the Western mass media. I retorted that the Party had left us no alternative, and that I did not retract a single point in my basic argument. He could see he was making no headway and left as amicably as he had come. The other point of his visit, of course, had been to check on what my interrogator had been saying about me.

What happened then?

The interrogation was virtually over by that time, and I continued to work on my written statement.

I ought to mention another dilemma that arose at this point. The interviews in the appendix to my dissertation were based on conversations with 48 university graduates, but only some eighty per cent of what I had put down came from the interviews themselves. The rest I had written up on the basis of earlier discussions, when the people in question, including myself, had not thought that the material would be used. When I came to write up the interviews, under anonymous headings like 'Engineer, 39, Head of Department', I saw no harm in altering things here and there, since the interviews were intended simply as illustrations of certain problems, not as evidence for my conclusions. But I can see now that this wasn't the proper thing to do. Besides, the degree of detail was not really compatible with anonymity, so that the security people must have thought I was an agent provocateur sent to worm out information for sale in the West. I tried to put these things out of my mind and I was naive enough to believe that they would not violate the anonymity. That's the way I am. They visited twenty of these people, put the fear of God into them, and got sworn statements to the effect that I had deliberately distorted their replies. Five of them were eventually called as witnesses at my trial. Let me tell you how it went.

In one of those interviews a man had told me that a particular factory was to be closed down and its products manufactured in Hungary instead. He now denied that he had said any such thing.

Did you see his statement beforehand?

Yes, I saw all these statements in advance and had to respond to them. I stuck to my guns and repeated that I had not falsified the interviews. The man then retracted part of his denial and said that he had simply forgotten about the plans to transfer production to Hungary. He went on to confirm that the account of the interview was basically accurate.

Was he the first witness?

Yes. Then came the second, who virtually denied that he had ever been interviewed at all, and cooked up crazy alibis that embarrassed even the rather crude and dim-witted prosecutor. The other three confirmed their statements in the main, only questioning the precise words or other minor points of detail. But, as I said, when I look back, I realize I should not have made it all so personal, especially as the themes could have been discussed without such individual references. I also took some responsibility for their answers, of course, since I addressed them in the form of leading questions that were far from neutral. If I were to see these men again today, I would feel a need to try to explain everything to them. It is a good thing for the whole moral situation in the GDR that these witnesses appeared in court. Apart from the one who lost his nerve—I really feel sorry for him—they all stood up for themselves. My lawyer was able to cross-question them, and even the judge was quite objective in critically examining their evidence. Unlike the prosecutor, he was a highly intelligent man. Considering that not everything had been proven, he probably used his own initiative to cut a year off the nine-year sentence demanded by the prosecution. Things were done as correctly as possible, no doubt with an eye to the outside world. My two letters published in *Der Spiegel* contain further details.

It was emphasized that my opinions were not on trial, but this did not stop them producing statements from various professors and institutions against my book and dissertation. In the Stalin era some of these statements would have sufficed to have me shot, especially those which quoted West German papers to show the harm I had done to the GDR. One of the men who had negatively assessed my dissertation at the time of its submission now came out with the accusation that I was a counter-revolutionary.

Was the compromise they offered you in November a real compromise or just a sham?

Well, after they saw that their usual methods would not extract any information and that I was open to the idea of a political compromise, they began to discuss things in these terms. A real compromise, of course, would have actually allowed me some scope for political activity.

What happened between the ostensible compromise in November and the general's visit in May?

They went through everything again in detail, especially the interviews appended to the dissertation, and I made it clear that I wasn't prepared to budge an inch. I put everything down in writing, page after page, including my views on how reforms that avoided the mistakes of the Czechoslovak Communist Party could be brought about under the guidance of the SED. When it came to the trial itself, the main evidence was just pieces taken from the book and quite grotesquely presented as information for the imperialists. Even the judge realized that much of this had been distorted and ripped out of context.

Did they refer to your television interviews?

No. They were never mentioned.

What about your interview with Der Spiegel?

That only came up because *Der Spiegel* was suspected of being involved in espionage and working hand-in-glove with Western intelligence.

How long did the whole trial last?

Two complete days. The terse verdict was delivered at the end of the week, in the morning.

Apart from the five people you interviewed, how many witnesses were called at the trial?

There were two other witnesses: my friend Ursula Benicke, and my best friend, the one who helped me most in the final stages of my book.

What was the maximum sentence for the charge of espionage?

I think it was ten years. I had reckoned on six, and I was surprised it was so stiff. But my whole case really proves that there is no need to be particularly afraid of them, and that one ought to be prepared to risk such confrontations with the Politbureau dictatorship.

One thing that many Communists in the West don't understand is why, knowing what a bad impression it would make on the outside world, they put you on trial at all and then sentenced you to eight years in jail.

I don't think they had any alternative. If they had done nothing, they would have given a green light to activities of the same kind. Since they did not want to convict me on ideological grounds, their only technical problem was to arrange as severe a sentence as possible on the spying charge. They were hardly interested at all in the opinions of Western Communists. Everything followed a perfectly logical course, attracting the maximum attention to their reactionary position. And that was a good thing.

But they wouldn't have been so stupid as not to anticipate this.

In the Soviet Union the regime is too thick-skulled properly to understand what goes on outside. In the GDR they are too narrowminded, too servile, too crabbed in their thinking. They have the sort of primitive authoritarian attitude that an old-fashioned father has towards his child—any attempt to answer back results in punishment. I am sure they didn't like doing what they did, and some Party leaders like Kurt Hager must have asked the questions you have just raised. But the Politbureau's sense of insecurity outweighs their capacity for rational political decisions.

So, after the trial you were taken straight to Bautzen prison.

No, no. My lawyer and I began to plan an appeal against the numerous legal errors in the judgement. This was rejected on the ground that eight years was justified by the seriousness of the offence. I spent another month in the cell in Berlin, and was then transferred to Bautzen.

How were conditions in Bautzen?

The jail consists almost entirely of single cells, each barely six or seven square metres in area. In former times, I heard, they even squeezed two men into a cell. I was isolated like this for about a month, but I soon made contact with other prisoners. They knew that I was coming because they had read about the case in the prison's copies of *Neues Deutschland*.

Were any other papers or journals available?

I was able to read the foreign news journal *Horizont*, the Moscow bilingual *Neue Zeit*, and various social-science and scientific periodicals.

What work did you have to do?

At first I had to thread spring clips on to screws; then I was put in a working party.

What were the other prisoners there for?

Most of them had been convicted of crimes with political overtones.

Some had engaged in black-market currency deals and been given sentences out of all proportion to their offence. Others had been caught trying to escape to the West and others still had worked for the security people and fallen from grace for one reason or another. A few prisoners, who seemed to have relatives in high places, were there not so much for reasons of privilege as because the authorities feared they might reveal embarrassing details about the regime to ordinary prisoners. In short, there were all kinds of people who had to be closely guarded.

The general ambience corresponded to my image of a well-run jail in the Weimar Republic. I came across no maltreatment, although people told me that before the Helsinki Agreements 'non-cooperators' had been subject to brutalities, and I have since been reliably informed that such treatment is still practised in some GDR prisons. The prison staff behaved correctly and the majority were quite good-humoured. Very rarely did they go beyond the letter of their orders. Unless a prisoner protested in a loud voice or became violent, he would generally be left to his own devices.

What especially irritated me were the senseless routines like roll call, because the warder knew perfectly well who was in each cell. And when we were let out, we had to fall in like soldiers. Before the penal code was reformed after the Helsinki Conference, prisoners were exercised in the yard in single file and were not allowed to talk. But when I was in Bautzen, the members of a working party were free to talk to one another. Each party was kept apart from the others, but illegal letters found their way backwards and forwards, in spite of the attentions of security men and informers.

How many prisoners were there in Bautzen altogether?

Between 100 and 150, I would say.

All male?

No, there were some women in a separate wing. We were able to speak to them across the yard in the evenings, even exchanging suitably guarded political remarks.

The really depressing thing was the fundamental injustice of the whole situation and the arbitrary power of the State Security. There was a young rowdy, for example, who had been given eleven years for some smuggling offence and for accepting money from the West. Prison made him into a serious political offender, but in fact he was a nobody and posed no danger to the state. He was the sort of man they could later use as an informer.

Were you allowed any visitors?

Before the trial I could have one visitor once a month for half an hour, and in Bautzen for one hour every two months. The whole system was very backward, and my former wife was the only person they let me see. Later, my children were also able to visit me.

Was there a prison library?

Yes. I used it to learn French, as well as for other things.

Were there classes? Or did you have to do everything by yourself?

By myself, of course. Every prisoner was allowed to study something, and I chose French. Some who were interested in classical music were allowed to listen to records for two hours every fortnight, and sometimes they brought the record player into my cell with some of these records. Then there were the books from the library. I ordered a copy of the Bible, which I had wanted to read for some time. (In Hohenschönhausen they had repeatedly turned down my request for a Bible, although they might have given me one if I had been a practising Christian.) You may be interested to know that I was also able to read Guardini's *The Lord*, a Catholic book.

Were you allowed to go to the library yourself or did they bring you the books to your cell?

I was given a list of all the books available and ordered what I wanted. Apart from the Christian books, there was a materialist history of the early Church, and a GDR book called *Figures of the Age of Bismarck* which dealt not only with Marx, Engels,

Liebknecht and so on but also with the other political parties. It was all from a Marxist point of view, of course, but with a good deal of interesting biographical information. Then I read for the first time Franz Mehring's *History of German Social Democracy*, and some classical literature, such as Goethe's *Wilhelm Meister*. The library was not at all bad for general cultural purposes, and there was technical material too, such as the language records I mentioned.

Were you expected to work very hard?

Once they had allocated me to a working party, in early September, I deliberately worked so hard that I exceeded the norm by two hundred per cent. People worked hard, not because of the pressure on them but in order to earn money to send home or to buy the few things available in the prison shop—butter, sausage, sweets, coffee, sometimes jam and fruit. The lack of vitamins was the worst aspect of both Berlin and Bautzen. In Berlin we had been fenced in with barbed wire, and the most we could see, from one corner of the exercise yard, was a second building and more barbed wire. In Bautzen at least one could see a few trees.

Were you allowed to write?

Only when I moved to Bautzen. I jotted down various political ideas, but someone informed on me and they confiscated it all. My first letter from Bautzen had been published while I was in solitary confinement, and I knew that the second letter had also since appeared. After the first, they went through all the papers and books in my cell, including a few my ex-wife had brought me. I had made notes on publications of the Institute for International Politics and Economics—the body that had provided a damning report on my dissertation—and also on articles from a Church journal, because I had the idea of writing something on the subject of Christ. But they took everything away.

I threatened to go on hunger strike in protest, pointing out that I had obeyed prison regulations to the letter and done my work properly. When they still refused to give my papers back, it became clear to me that they were acting on instructions from Berlin. I had already deliberately asked my lawyer to obtain permission for me to receive certain publications that went well beyond what was customary. But they denied me many of these, including *L'Humanité*, and only let me read books out of the prison library. What they were out to stop was that I would publish anything else like the *Spiegel* letters.

Were you ever taken to task over these letters?

No, never. Twice the security people came down from Berlin, but they were only out to see what I would say to them. They just asked what I was doing with myself, and I replied that there wasn't much I could do, since they had locked me up safely.

So, you never managed to read L'Humanité?

Once or twice I did, but through another prisoner. When I asked for access to a typewriter and a radio, it was not surprisingly turned down. But I was determined to take things to the limit. The day before I was due to begin my hunger-strike, I wrote a long and bitter letter to the Chief State Prosecutor, hoping it would find its way out of the prison. But one of the links in the chain must have been a plant, and it ended up with the State Security. Still, I was never punished for my action.

I started the hunger-strike on 11 January, the day after the doctor had told me I was too much of an intellectual for such an action. He was a good doctor, who behaved very correctly towards me, but he was completely non-political and really believed I would not stick it out.

For one day they let me stay in the working party. Then they isolated me in a dark hole that ought to have been done away with long ago, far worse than anything the security police would have used in Berlin. There were cobwebs in the corners and thick wire-mesh over the glass tile window. There was no table or wash-basin, only a toilet and a tap, and the stable lamp over the door had wire-mesh to protect it against people who went berserk. I realized that the doctor had to keep an eye on me, and he or his assistant came regularly and took my pulse and blood pressure and so on. I was given my customary leisure period and allowed to see *Neues*

Deutschland, but nothing else apart from one copy of *Horizont.*
After six days in that black hole, I was taken to the doctor to be force-fed. He was sure I would give up my hunger-strike on the spot. I only lost some ten pounds in weight and was in better shape than other prisoners told me they had been on an empty stomach. I had continued to take a certain amount of exercise, and that must certainly have helped. I felt a bit dizzy if I got up too quickly, but otherwise felt no particular complaints. I also drank a lot of liquid, as the others had told me to do.

Anyway, they put the tube in my mouth and tried to feed me. I pulled it out, but two policemen held me from behind and the tube was forced in.

They used to do that in hospitals before the First World War, but they had to give it up because the patients became frantic.

They had no choice but to force-feed me. After my first, symbolic struggle, I could see that they were determined to go ahead with it, and they started to tie me down and give me injections. The doctor wasn't a brutal man by nature. He was the director of Bautzen 1 hospital, and also had responsibility for Bautzen 2, a huge place with something between two and four thousand patients. I thought they might put me in Bautzen 1 or transfer me to Leipzig, but they carried it all out where I was.

Shortly after that first attempt, I heard a sudden loud noise on the next floor down. It turned out that they were preparing a more decent cell for my 'treatment', one with windows barred on the inside and outside to make it more difficult to communicate with anyone across the yard. As soon as I found myself in the new cell, I naturally climbed up to look out of the window. A guard had been peeping through the door, waiting for me to do just this, and he rushed in and nailed up the window in such a way as to let the air enter but to prevent me from calling to anyone outside. Nevertheless, I did somehow manage to make myself heard. I kept up my hunger-strike for thirty-one days, so that they must have fed me through the tube for a total of twenty-five days. The doctor came to see me forty times. I have no complaints over this aspect of my treatment. I had brought the situation on myself, and they had to see that nothing happened to me. Apart from the force-feeding, they gave me injections for two weeks.

When I found out that my letter to the Chief State Prosecutor had not left the prison, I decided to abandon the hunger-strike. During the last few days, the doctor had begun to show signs of impatience and made the treatment more unpleasant by leaving a thinner tube in my nose. But it was not done out of viciousness. The doctor told me that if I had given up the strike, it would have been a feather in his own cap. He also told me—and I believed him—that it weighed on his own conscience to be treating me like that. He would rather have spent his time on his proper patients. Yet he understood why I was doing what I did, even as he kept telling me there was no point. I didn't know that the second letter I had smuggled out of Bautzen had been published in the meantime. This obviously gave them more reason to keep me secluded.

I was in solitary confinement for a total of four months, from 10 January until the end of April. I don't think they were being especially spiteful in isolating me like this, but they were glad to be able to use the pretext of special medical treatment. Two weeks after I ended the strike they brought me work to do as before. I also began to receive books again. During my hunger-strike I had read the Bible and studied a lot of French.

They moved me upstairs into a cell next to the one I had been in before. It wasn't as bad as the black hole, but it only had glass tiles instead of a proper window.

The noises started again on the floor below me, and I later found out they were preparing a whole special section. When I was taken down at the end of April, there was already another man in the cell—a police plant. A war criminal who had been involved in the mass murder of Jews in the Ukraine was brought in later. He was a typical SA man from a working-class background, who said he had only done what he did because he would have been shot if he had refused.

That's what they all said.

He had been given twenty-five years by the Russians at the end of the war, but was released long before his term was up. He returned to the GDR without saying a word, and it was only much later that they caught up with him. And there he sat next to me in front of the television—we had one in our cell—and repeated all the official talk about the interests of the working class and so on.

Did you stay in the cell until you were released?

Yes. There was always a special guard on duty, and throughout my leisure period a man stood by me to ensure that I made no contact with anyone else. I did, however, talk to people across the yard. And they allowed me to have French gramophone records.

They knew that Bautzen wasn't secure, and these precautions were designed to prevent me smuggling out another letter. The special area was completely open, so that I could go and play cards with the other two if I wanted. In theory I did a full day's work, five days a week, 8¾ hours a day, but in practice I only worked five hours and my output was low. They knew I was probably spending the time doing something else. They had closed-circuit television, although it gave a very bad picture and didn't tell them much. The informer knew everything I did and naturally passed it on, but they did not seem to care. There was one bath for the three of us, and in spite of my low standard of work I was allowed to watch the English and Russian-language programmes twice a week.

For a whole month I used to call across the yard in French to one of the other prisoners, but they never actually caught me at it. When I was hauled before the warden, he said they didn't want to take things to extremes, and nor should I. I had the feeling they wanted to keep up this sort of contact with me.

The security people visited me twice after my hunger-strike. The first time, immediately afterwards, they found me just as I had always been, completely relaxed, and asked whether anything had changed. The second time, after I had been transferred to the new cell in the special section, they asked me whether I had any information I wanted them to pass to the West. When I replied that in any case they wouldn't pass it on, they assured me that they certainly would.

How far were you in the picture about the campaign for your release?

I learned nothing through official channels, but the West German prisoners (some, but not all, real agents) had access to the West German Communist paper *Unsere Zeit* and its West Berlin equivalent, *Die Wahrheit*. Before I arrived, there had also been a Swiss citizen who received copies of *Vorwärts* and it was through these means that people knew about the discussion of my book. I wrote down its main principles again and distributed them to certain of my fellow-prisoners. Some were a little suspicious because I made it clear that I was still a Communist; and when they found out that I had the confidence of quite varied people, they began to think I might be a security agent myself. But although the Springer press made me out to be a double agent, they soon realized there was no truth in it.

Did you know there had been a Bahro Meeting in Berlin?

Yes. Someone also called through the window that there had been a similar event in Marburg.

Would you now tell us a little about the circumstances of your release.

The first sign was a TV report about an amnesty. I was more than fifty-per-cent certain that I would be included, because it was an ideal opportunity to get rid of me without leaving the impression that they were yielding to outside pressure. They could just let me out with the rest. Meanwhile, I had thought things over and made it clear in my letter from prison that I was prepared to consider going to the West.

Was this your own initiative? Did anyone suggest that this was a possibility?

After the trial, while I was waiting for the appeal to be heard, the prosecutor told me that Klaus Bölling, the West German government spokesman, had said that the Federal Republic was prepared to accept me. But it was my own decision: there was no longer any political purpose in remaining in the GDR.

Just before the thirtieth anniversary of the GDR, they turned my cell upside down again in search of the things they knew I had been writing. Then, on the second day of the amnesty, 11 October, I was hurriedly released. They put a piece of paper in front of me with two conditions: that I should have no contact with the West German media; and that I should make official application to leave the GDR. My lawyer thought it would take weeks to deal with such an application, so I told him to tell them to hurry, in case I started talking with West German journalists again. I was sure they wouldn't risk putting me in jail a second time.

After my release, I first went to see my ex-wife and children. She wasn't there but the children were. Barely a quarter of an hour later, two journalists from *Stern* magazine appeared on the scene. They were decent chaps, however, and they agreed not to take any photographs or to report immediately that they had seen me.

I had been constantly watched on the journey from Bautzen to Dresden, then from Dresden to Berlin. But now things were going too far: whole squads of cars were parked outside the house, outside Uschi's house, outside my friends' houses, all with two or three men inside. I knew they couldn't keep it up for long.

I went to my local town hall in Weissensee, in Berlin, and handed in my application for an exit permit. The woman in charge wasn't really prepared for me. Not only was she surprised to find me a person whose whole attitude corresponded to the ethos of the GDR, but she was clearly worried about accepting an application which impudently claimed that my book had contributed to the country's development. Still, she did eventually accept it: she was a good woman, very correct, and she even sent away a security agent loitering outside the door. 'It's alright, he's with me now', she told him. I later sent her a bunch of flowers in gratitude.

The authorities now had to find me somewhere to live, since they couldn't publicly admit that I was going to leave the country. It began to seem that they couldn't find me a furnished flat at such short notice, and in a way I was glad that they couldn't. It didn't quite seem right. But in the end they did find me something. When I went to Eisenhüttenstadt to say goodbye to my mother, it became clear to me that everything was being done to arrange a quiet departure. I was allowed to see whomever I wanted to see, and someone even came to visit me from Robert Havemann.

As chance would have it, my Aunt Hertha from West Germany was visiting my mother at that time. This could have caused difficulties, because she would have told everyone about me when she got back. But when I called at my mother's, I found that she was visiting friends outside town. Although the house was surrounded by cars, she simply hadn't known I was coming.

I then hired a taxi to take me to her friend's house, but the police kept me waiting until another two cars could make up my compulsory four-car escort. Still, I finally managed to see my mother and say farewell.

When I returned to Berlin that evening, I thought I would try to see Havemann before I left. Up to then I had been allowed to see anyone I liked—the security men just waited outside. I knew there would be Western journalists near Havemann's house, but I didn't want to have any dealings with them, and nor did I want to provoke the authorities.

I was sure they would let me see Havemann, but the next day they told me it was out of the question. I said I would not leave until I had seen him, arguing that, after all, we were both Communists and that it could do no harm. As they knew, Havemann even wanted me to stay in the GDR. But they were adamant. By the Tuesday evening all the arrangements had been made for my departure, and on the morning of Wednesday, 17 October, four security cars drove us to the border at Marienborn. I was in one of the cars alone with my lawyer. Uschi was in the second car, and my ex-wife and children in a third; the fourth must have been empty. At Marienborn they put us all on the train, watching us down to the last moment.

There was another man, a friend of Havemann's, whom I had tried to see when it became obvious that I wouldn't be able to speak to Havemann himself. But after we had exchanged a few words, the security men intervened and stood between us. I then gave up the attempt.

How many other prisoners were released from Bautzen?

I just don't know. I was the first, and from odd scraps of information I have gleaned since then, I would say there were only two more. It all depended on the whim and fancy of the security police, and certain people were excluded from the amnesty who ought not to have been.

4
Facing The Global Crisis

What were the main thoughts in your mind when you decided to come to the West?

My reasoning was more or less as follows. If I left, the ideas presented in my book could be divorced from my own person and would have to be discussed in an ideological context as such. The regime was still in a position to isolate people like Havemann from the majority of thinking Party members, whereas if I were no longer there, the apparatchiks could not claim that I was lurking behind any expression of such ideas. Besides, no colleague could ever allow himself to be seen with me.

I also thought that if I were able to have some influence on the left wing of West German politics, it could help to strengthen the position of those in the GDR who wanted to discuss such matters. A number of comrades there have recently said as much, hoping that I will stick to my guns in the West and make clear that I am still a communist.

If I had stayed there, I could somehow have managed to live in a freelance capacity. Life isn't so expensive in the GDR, and I could have existed on five hundred marks a month. It would also have been a less strenuous life than here in the West. I planned to write a book in which I would examine the whole phenomenon of Marxism under the heading of Ethics, as Spinoza did with the philosophical system of his day. *The Alternative* amounts to a direct confrontation with the official line. But having made my point, I wouldn't have kept up that degree of confrontation, although nor would I have retracted anything. I always conceived of a semi-legal political existence for myself in the GDR, like those Hungarian Communists who manage to retain some sort of independent line. I would have regarded that as productive for the future political development of the country.

In the second chapter of your book, where you deal with the origins of the non-capitalist road in Russia and other post-capitalist or 'proto-socialist' countries, you talk of it as a road which started from the ground not of socialism, but of a predominantly pre-capitalist development. You say, for example, that the revolution in Russia, China, the Balkans or Cuba greatly contributed to universal progress by creating its own industrial base, its own working class, and so on.

Above all, as Frantz Fanon said, it is better if these peoples follow such a course through their own efforts than with the help of social-democratic growth experts.

That's very well put. In any case, these are countries which had to extricate themselves from an earlier pre-capitalist form of development. Things were quite different in the GDR, which had its industrial revolution in the nineteenth century. What would be your general balance-sheet of the GDR's development?

I said in my book that I regarded the development of the GDR as uncharacteristic. It is impossible to understand relations in those countries by reference to them alone. The real theoretical problem is that although an external, Russian construct was clamped on them, a basic continuity remained in the development of the productive forces that stemmed from the capitalist industrial system.

But how would you situate the GDR in the general course of German and European history? It is also, of course, the most developed socialist country.

Perhaps not much more developed than Czechoslovakia.

But it did not go through the experience of 1968, which was followed by a catastrophic moral laceration of the whole Czechoslovak state.

Yes. That is a very important difference. Anyway, the GDR economy is obviously not on the brink of collapse: although it has scarcely any raw materials of its own and is undermined by a lack of efficiency, it is still a basically stable structure. The GDR's reserves for mobilization are being eroded by the bureaucratic system itself, but this is clearly a gradual process.

There are also a number of historical considerations. People forget that the fragmentation of Germany after the Thirty Years War led to an intensification not only of exploitation but also of culture in the widest sense. The rulers were so close to those they held down that a kind of paternalism remained until well into the nineteenth century. I doubt whether the typically German qualities of diligence, orderliness and the like would have developed if the rulers had lived elsewhere in the manner of absentee landlords, or if a remote, inefficient bureaucracy had wielded a strongly centralized power. The differences between the large states—Russia, Austria, Bavaria—and the numerous smaller states also brought a beneficial dynamism into the system. These aspects of the German national character show themselves in the GDR today, where capitalist productive forces have shown themselves to be far from incompatible with the Soviet style of economic planning. I have referred to this phenomenon as 'factory despotism' at the level of society as a whole. Indeed, as far as work organization and managerial functions are concerned, I can even see analogies between the building of Magnitogorsk and the building of the Pyramids.

Would that also hold for the building of Eisenhüttenstadt, Schwarze Pumpe and other new industrial centres in the GDR?

Of course the whole analogy should be taken with a pinch of salt. But although the more developed conditions in the GDR required some understanding with the mass of subordinate workers, so that forced labour was never a major form as in Stalin's Russia, the fact remains that the relations of domination associated with factory despotism were the basic form of social organization. If the Soviet pattern could be clamped on the GDR economy, it was essentially because the old division of labour continued to function, albeit with a different emphasis. Kautsky's mechanistic theory, which certainly influenced Soviet leaders, was that one had only to lop off German capitalism and militarism, so to speak, and one would be left with the roots of socialism. At the same time, it should be stressed that 'actually existing socialism' did not develop organically within the GDR or Czechoslovakia. There was nothing like the Russian Revolution there, no fundamental upheaval that came from the roots. It was the defeat of Hitler in 1945 that made a completely new pattern of development possible. But if the Marshall Plan had been extended to East Germany, as it was then known, the bourgeoisie would have come to the fore again and all the efforts of comrades newly released from concentration camps would not have been enough to thwart a capitalist restoration.

You imply that developments in the GDR have led into a cul-de-sac. How do you reconcile this with what you said in your letter from Bautzen, that you support the non-capitalist principles of the GDR and seek a political and ideological way forward on the basis of those principles?

In world-historical terms, what I say about the non-capitalist foundation applies to Eastern Europe as a whole. The GDR is not an end in itself, any more than Czechoslovakia is. As I see it, the GDR has had the task of preserving the qualitative aspect of the Soviet industrial process. Naturally this brings with it certain limitations in efficiency from the national point of view. For it makes a difference whether your economic production is linked to the USA or to the Soviet Union: one has only to look at Austria to see the truth of that. But from a broader, non-nationalist perspective, the evolution of the GDR or Czechoslovakia must be seen in the light of that fateful meeting of the Russians and Americans at the Elbe in 1945. After all, Nazism was not a self-contained phenomenon but a manifestation of the confrontation that started with the Russian Revolution—the revolution that I regard as the forerunner for the process of industrialization in a second, non-capitalist world.

If, as you say, the GDR is a kind of service-station for Soviet industry, then Germany history would appear to have no meaning.

In a sense the history of Germany as a self-conscious nation did come to an end in 1945. But, however sharply I may criticize the Soviet Union, it is a fact of great significance that the existence of the GDR prevented the old capitalist system from being re-established in the whole of Germany. Another result is that in the GDR—things are rather different in the Federal Republic—there has been a near-total break with the old militarist, imperialist Nazi tradition. The comical military parades on the Unter den Linden may evoke, psychologically, a certain sense of continuity, but in all ideological and political respects the past has been swept away.

In the second part of your book, you argue that the capitalist countries have proved more effective in raising labour productivity, and some of the things you have been saying today also point to that conclusion. However, apart from the obvious waste apparent in the 18 to 20 million unemployed in the advanced capitalist countries, you do not seem to take into account that the growth-rate of the economy is still considerably higher in the socialist countries—twice as high in the USSR as in the USA, even over the last ten years.

To some extent I discuss this in connection with the achievements of Stalin's Russia. But we should be clear what we are talking about. If I put three sacks of coal alongside two mini-computers, I could say that the sacks of coal represent a greater increase in production than the computers. But it would be a false argument. There's obviously an economic gap, a growing gap, between the GDR and West Germany: the West is always at least one step ahead. One cannot say that developments in the GDR and Czechoslovakia prove the superiority of the other system, although many people, both in the GDR and the Federal Republic, would say that they did.

Now, my positive evaluation of the non-capitalist base of the Eastern bloc rests on two fundamental points. First, the relations of command are much easier to establish than in the capitalist system. Secondly, and perhaps even more important, the problems facing our civilization require centralized social planning if they are to be solved, and this aspect must not be abandoned in the necessary changes in Eastern Europe. It is always possible to discuss whether the market has a role to play in satisfying the needs of the population, but the general proportions of the reproduction process must be planned. There has to be a change in our whole system of production, for technology in the present-day world carries the capitalist mode of reproduction within itself.

The root of the problem in the countries of 'actually existing socialism' is that the political structure necessarily involves a discrepancy between accumulation and consumption. I do not believe that any variant of the capitalist market economy could have matched the industrial construction achieved in the first phase of Russia's post-revolutionary development, and the Soviet Union would not have been capable of militarily defending itself without the high rate of accumulation of the 1930s. However, the political structure which made that possible is not the best suited to carry through the transition to intensive production, especially in view of the challenge from the West and the fact that Russia never extended its influence in the Pacific. The decline in the Soviet growth-rate to less than four per cent is a clear argument against the present political-economic structures.

The population in the GDR, then, knows, or at least thinks, that there is a growing industrial gap between their country and the Federal Republic. It is also aware of the lack of normal bourgeois-democratic freedoms. Does this mean that they are strongly opposed to the present state in the GDR?

On the basis of my impressions of several Western countries, I should first say that the same extremes of rich and poor are not found in the GDR—except, perhaps, in the case of old-age pensioners, whose position is still not satisfactory. If I had to make a comparison, I would say that the average person lives better in the GDR than in Italy. It has been said that living standards in the GDR are some twenty-five per cent below those in West Germany. But since the Federal Republic is one of the richest countries in the world, the GDR must also be comparatively wealthy. There is sometimes a problem of quality, but the bulk of material goods are in adequate supply.

More important than the quality or quantity of consumer goods, in my view, is the need for a new consumption pattern geared to the *qualitative* development of the individual, so that the length of young people's education, for example, becomes a higher priority than the addition of one more piece of clothing to my wardrobe.

For luxuries that are in short supply, there is a sort of black market in the GDR in which one product is bartered against another. As in the Soviet Union, you have to know who has what, and to be able to offer something in return. There is also a general shortage of spare parts. Housing is still the biggest problem; but if not by 1990, as promised, then by 1995 there will be sufficient decent accommodation for everybody. Already quite a number of people even have a little cottage in the country as well as their town flat, and some of these places are very comfortably equipped.

So far you have only talked about material conditions. What is the general attitude to the regime and to the West?

The strongest influence, allied to lower productivity and the resulting lower standard of living, is the consumption-oriented model of West Germany. However, the majority of working people in the GDR are well aware that labour intensity and competitive pressures are far greater in the West, so they end up wanting the consumer goods but not the capitalist system. Most of the old-age pensioners who visit the West say that everything is fine and rosy, but that they wouldn't like to live there for good.

Many people also realize, perhaps without expressing it in so many words, that the lower productivity and standard of living in the GDR are due not only to faults in planning but also to the low morale of workers, who know they are not giving of their best. There is a great deal of timewasting, and since no material pressure can be brought to bear on them, the workers are just subjected to a barrage of verbal injunctions and pressures. Certainly there is an increasing sense of demoralization, but people generally feel that no campaign of protest or anything else is going to change a situation that is ultimately defended by Soviet tanks.

There is a great tendency for people in the GDR to keep out of political matters. Offended by the continual repetition of the same old official sermon, they just stop listening. What really annoys them is the way they are made to say 'yes' in a mockery of the democratic process like local elections. Everybody has to cast their vote so as to produce one hundred per cent approval, and even if you are on your death-bed, they will turn up at your house with the ballot-box.

Then, of course, there is the Wall. People naturally want to see for themselves what the West is like, although most of them would come back again. At the same time, there is a small but significant proportion of highly skilled people at the height of their productive capacity who simply feel unable to fulfil their potential in the GDR and would not return from the West. It's not a matter of the higher living standards but of the opportunity for self-fulfilment, the freedom to leave one realm of activity for another until one finds the greatest success and satisfaction. If people like this were allowed to leave, the country would suffer and the state would in practice be financing capitalism. As I see it, therefore, the first task of a Dubček-type regime in the GDR would not be to pull down the Wall. We would need to find a way of making it unnecessary, so that the average person would be free to visit the West because he would be sure to come back. But that is the very opposite of the official mentality, which operates on the basis of an almost totally irrational suspicion. I have the impression that the State Security sets itself an annual target of arrests for contact with the West. If they don't, the men in the Politbureau say: 'What's happening? Are you losing your vigilance in the class struggle? Or are you becoming less efficient?' So they put together a case against some insignificant person or other—the petty fiddler in Bautzen, for example, who had taken away some food and drink left over from a reception at the Austrian Embassy. Perhaps he should have been given two years, but they gave him eleven for accepting bribes from the West. After he was released in a general amnesty, he was so softened up that they were easily able to use him as an informer.

How would you describe the general attitude to the question of democratic freedoms?

What I have been saying about the ban on travel to the West applies to the whole population. But the intelligentsia in the broadest sense of the term—including, that is, any thinking worker—is particularly interested in questions of democracy. It is not so much the bourgeois electoral mechanism that concerns them as the possiblity of exerting some influence over economic planning and political life. They naturally resent being spoon-fed by the state information monopoly, which prevents them from forming their own opinions and having any say on various national and international questions. The sense of frustration is strongest of all among social scientists, who are well informed and at best cynically resigned to the system.

My general position on the GDR, which we have been discussing at a theoretical level, is basically shared by most of the Party membership. We are all against capitalism, and we have achieved something in the GDR that works, even if it doesn't always work all that well, and even if we keep telling one another anecdotes about the way things go wrong. As to the ordinary people, some will declare their allegiance to the Party or the state, while others are neutral and a small minority actually reject the regime. Owing to their psychological structure, an even smaller group feel so outraged at the whole system..:

Is theirs really a psychological reaction, rather than a class position?

The old class positions really have very little to do with it. There are fewer such people left in the GDR than in any other East European country, for the simple reason that most of them went to the West. Although only the regime has precise information, I would say that the small number of people who violently hate the system come from all social classes, including the working class, or at least people who are workers by current occupation. But as I said before, most people don't want a return to capitalism, and nor do they want all the upheaval that would be necessary for Germany to become a united country again. They know that the stability of the GDR is inseparable from peace and stability in Europe as a whole, so that most of them eventually came round to accepting the Soviet invasion of Czechoslovakia, for example. Even if something were to 'happen' in the GDR, it would never come to open war. The mass of the population are afraid.

One has the impression that the regime attempts to foster a kind of GDR patriotism, which expresses itself in sport and so on, with a certain anti-West-German content. How successful is this policy?

Of course I do not have the sociological data to give you a precise answer. But there are 1.6 million members of the Socialist Unity Party, including passive elements who may at most be considered loyal to the Party. Then there are many other people who remain loyal to the state. Among all these sections, then, you find a generally positive or loyal attitude to the regime, although 'GDR patriotism' is probably too strong a term. Finally, there is quite a large group of people who have a neutral attitude: for example, the women in factories and offices who used to say to me that they weren't against the regime, but that it was unable to give them many of the things they wanted, including the dismantling of the Wall and the freedom to travel. But despite their criticisms, they have stuck by the GDR in the end. And, in their different ways, so have people like Robert Havemann, Stefan Heym, Erich Löst, the singer Bettina Wegener, and Klaus Schlesinger. So, in a way, have I.

Is this loyalty to the GDR partly due to a kind of resentment of West Germany?

Partly, yes. You find that workers will grouse and swear about conditions when they are in their factory, but when some well-heeled uncle arrives on a visit from West Germany, they stand up for the GDR and point out all the good things about it, all the disadvantages they had to overcome after 1945, and so on. Although the state's demands for loyalty are widely resented, I would say that in normal, crisis-free times there is a sufficiently high degree of loyalty to assure the country's stability.

In the last fifteen years the economic situation in the GDR has greatly improved and the country has gained international recognition. What effect have these two facts had?

The increase in international recognition has certainly boosted the sense of loyalty to the state, whereas the rise in living standards has made little difference, because the GDR still lags far behind West Germany. As far as the masses are concerned, it's still like the race between the hare and the hedgehog. People say that the state has given them this year what they should have had last year. And when they then read letters in *Neues Deutschland* thanking the Party for everything it has done, the whole thing becomes quite ludicrous. In fact, almost everyone connected with the propaganda machine knows that it functions in the most ludicrous manner. But the longer the country survives, commanding greater attention in the world, the more irreversible the fact of its existence becomes. The key point remains 13 August 1961—the day the Wall went up.

When I look back now, I can see that we haven't really progressed beyond the 13th of August and the circumstances that made it necessary. Thinking people like Havemann, Heym or Bahro—who are loyal to the state and, in the most general sense, to the Party—are precisely those who want to revolutionize the political system. The new contradictions are bringing about a destabilization—not, I hope, of the state but of apparatus rule. More and more people take no pleasure in what they do, even members of the apparatus itself, who do not have the majority of the population behind them and even have to rule against their passive resistance. If you wear your Party badge, you stick out like a sore thumb and people avoid you. Since they automatically assume that you will say what you have been programmed to say, they have to know you very well before they will openly express their views. What was possible in 1961, when nearly all Party members and many other people supported Ulbricht and the Wall, is no longer possible today. There is an irreversible process of disassociation from the Party apparatus, although the fact that the country is sandwiched between the Federal Republic and the Soviet Army makes it very difficult to say when this will take concrete shape.

How do the generations differ in their attitudes?

The older generation are generally content to stay there. Those who couldn't make their peace with the situation after the war left for the West while it was still possible, but the remainder do not feel that things are so fundamentally different from what they knew in the Weimar Republic, especially in the smaller towns. Life is not so hectic there: the regime leaves you more or less alone except when it comes to the wretched elections, when local bureaucrats drag everyone out to make up the ridiculous 99.8 per cent or whatever it is.

In the middle generation there are certainly people, including a proportion of dynamic and distinguished ones, who would probably take the chance to leave the GDR, if only because the chance might not return. Feeling unfulfilled and seeking a broader field in which to express themselves, they are more rational and more open to information and argument from outside than their parents. This is the generation which is now sustaining the GDR. The key positions are still held by the conformist type, like Comrade Wunschgetreu in the Strittmatter novel I mentioned at the beginning. But they will disappear in time.

Finally, there is a slightly younger generation who feel no responsibility for Nazism or the war and have a critical attitude towards the Soviet Union and the GDR. They are not critical in a negative sense, but they could not, as Honecker is said to have done, kiss the earth when they first set foot on Soviet soil. They have helped to build up the country and, in a non-emphatic sort of way, are basically patriotic towards it. Politically they would like to have a kind of Dubček regime in which they had some say, although they have resigned themselves to the fact that this is not possible. This was the generation of people I interviewed for my dissertation, and in most of them I could clearly sense an underlying resignation.

As to the new generation of young people, whose experience of socialism began after 1961, they have had no influence on the way things have developed. It was all ready-made when they arrived on the scene, and they were just expected to accept it all as it was laid down for them in school—laid down, I may add, by teachers who often don't believe it themselves. Yet here too, if there were a plebiscite on whether Germany as a whole should model itself on the GDR or the Federal Republic—not, of course, Honecker or Brandt—then most would vote for the GDR.

But they don't want a united Germany in any case.

They certainly consider the prospect illusory and do not want the risks that a struggle for reunification would involve. But it would be a different matter if a real possibility arose.

Don't they regard themselves as a distinctive socialist nation?

I don't understand that use of the word 'nation'. The younger generation is just as dissatisfied with its own ossified conditions as is its counterpart in the Federal Republic. They are just expected to get on with their work, or to excel in sport, as a kind of substitute for really helping to build up the country. All this competitive sport I find detestable and inhuman.

Surely sport is important for young people.

Only because they have no other outlet. Anyway, sport is not sufficient to conceal what is lacking elsewhere. The children of intellectuals, including those in the Party, are particularly critical of the system, but they also have the intelligence to shape their own attitudes and careers, whereas workers' children are just put off by the education they get, and negative tendencies tend to develop when they go out to work. The wage structure is another source of problems. For a skilled worker takes home more than young engineers, and yet tends to suspect them of belonging to 'the other side', to those who are responsible for the unsatisfactory conditions.

Just as in the capitalist countries.

Exactly. It is a product of the 'factory despotism' based upon the division between manual and intellectual labour. What Marx called 'the function of capital' has, in this narrow sense, not been reduced: capital remains in the GDR, although the concept 'state capitalism' is not, in my view, applicable. Anyway, the younger generation is harsher and less constructive in its criticism. My generation will undoubtedly be able to cooperate with it when things begin to change. But young people, who naturally want a root-and-branch reform overnight, will have to be shown that one cannot simply destroy the administrative apparatus without causing the whole organization of society to collapse. The relations of domination have to be done away with, but central regulatory mechanisms will obviously remain necessary. For where the market mechanism has ceased to play a significant role, one cannot simply proceed in accordance with the old aim of 'smashing the apparatus'.

Let us now come to another important aspect of your book. In the first part you concern yourself with the proto-socialist state, above all in pre-capitalist societies essentially unlike the GDR. In the third part you advance the programme for a cultural revolution based upon a highly developed system of industrial production, such as may exist in the GDR, but certainly not in the majority of proto-socialist countries like China, Vietnam or even the Soviet Union. Thus, you say that the cultural revolution should include a 'qualitatively simple reproduction', very slow and controlled forms of growth, yet 95 per cent of the populations that live in these countries still experience enormous material shortages. How can a programme of slow or zero growth be combined there with very advanced demands that point beyond, let us say, Fordism in the United States?

On the question of economic growth, I make it clear in my book that a gap needs to be bridged in the Soviet Union. But I firmly maintain that the people of the Soviet Union, or of Poland, will gain nothing if the present form of economic growth, which is simply a reactive extension of the capitalist form, is retained. You may say that the GDR needs houses. Certainly it does. But maybe we have reached the point where, even in highly developed countries, we should ask whether all houses need air conditioning, whether shoppers need automatic doors in department stores, and so on. If there were not a fully equipped modern house next door, we would still find Schiller's house in Weimar perfectly habitable. It's a question of what standards we apply.

Of course we need things like railways in Siberia—basics which have nothing to do with capitalism except in a historical sense. But what is necessary in one country is not necessary in another, and we cannot transfer the pattern to, say, Poland, let alone to the Third World countries or China. We can only hope that their vision of the good life is different from that in Washington, London and Paris.

You seem to be confusing two distinct questions: on the one hand, the model of needs and the goods produced; on the other, the rate of economic development. Surely the level of material deprivation is still so great that growth needs to be speeded up, not slowed down.

I have my doubts about that. The shortage of meat in Poland, for example, has nothing to do with the level of the productive forces but with the unresolved social contradictions.

Isn't it all part of the same problem? After all, Polish agriculture is still largely unmechanized: there are some three million horses on the land.

There are certainly connections, but it may be a good thing for those horses to remain. Only if too much labour-power is removed from the countryside will there necessarily be a shortage of meat in the huge agricultural expanse of Poland.

But when industrialization became necessary, workers left the land and can never go back.

Why did industrialization have to be carried through in that way? Only because it is part of the capitalist model. What can be done for 35 million people in Poland cannot be done for the eight billion on this planet. There simply aren't enough resources.

But the Poles aren't satisfied with their standard of living and would not like it to fall still further. Besides, it can be scientifically shown that the eight billion people you talk about could reach a higher standard than that of the Poles today.

But how long could they keep it up?

Alright. That is a question that needs to be tackled patiently and empirically. But let us return to your book. Do you think that the cultural revolution you write about in The Alternative *can be achieved in, say, Vietnam? Or were you essentially thinking of the GDR?*

My starting-point was that in the whole of Eastern Europe, including the Soviet Union, industrial development has to shift its emphasis from sheer quantity to quality, to what makes for a higher quality of life. The first question for me is not *whether* the cultural revolution is possible in China or Vietnam or wherever, but that it is essential. If this doesn't happen, then the capitalist type of growth will prevail and end in complete disaster. The sort of cultural revolution I describe must be our first priority, since that is what will enable us to use our material resources in a new way. Under the capitalist pattern we have assumed that man needs everything that capitalism offers him, needs more and ever more. The fact that the earth's resources are limited, like the earth itself, compels us to ask what man really needs for his development as a human being.

But if you are saying that the cultural revolution is applicable in Vietnam, how can you justify your position that Stalinist industrialization was necessary as the shortest road to socialism in Russia? Why was it necessary in 1930 and not today?

In 1917 Russia was faced with the world dominance of capitalist imperialism and it had no choice but to take over and expand the productive forces it had inherited. The same tendency is there today in Eastern Europe, as well as in the Third and the Fourth World, and it is this tendency that must be broken. We in the highly developed countries are in the front line. We must grab the chance to carry through a cultural revolution in the way that Mao tried to do in China, because we cannot live with the old system any longer.

Are you not conceding that the third part of your book is only applicable in the most highly developed states?

One of the reasons why my book has been so well received in the West may be that it seems more relevant to the Western situation. For it is here that the terrible treadmill is in operation and must be brought to a halt. But in the meantime we should not tell the peoples of Eastern Europe to go further along this path.

But what if they want to?

The Communist Parties there shouldn't give it their approval. I don't mean, of course, that the necessary Communist League should force through this cultural revolution, but that it should oppose the existing form of industrial progress in the way—to take an extreme analogy—that the Church opposed it at the end of the Middle Ages.

One other basic question arises in connection with the final part of your book. You argue for a uniform model of development all over the world, whereas historical materialism simply denies that such a thing can be voluntaristically created. It has always insisted that historical development is highly uneven, with different patterns of social, economic and political development in different material circumstances. To impose one model, drawn from one part of the world, on all other countries is a bureaucratic utopia. It is inconceivable that everything could conform to what may well be highly appropriate in our own countries.

That is a very interesting question. I have already argued elsewhere that we must look for the holes in historical materialism and try to tackle them in a serious manner. For it involves a theoretical abstraction from the natural-historical process, such that history is made to develop spontaneously in a law-like manner. This helpless sense of inevitability—the kind one feels when a swarm of locusts descends on an area of land and strips it bare—must be overcome if mankind is not to suffer a similar fate.

The starting-point for my whole book is that we have not yet succeeded in breaking through the horizon of capitalist civilization to reach the vision of a world-wide alternative. It is true that the peoples of the world are at different levels of development, but one has to make use of the concrete possibilities where the civilization is not so overdetermined by the capitalist productive forces. This is precisely why a cultural revolution should be welcomed in Vietnam, for example. The whole of mankind is moving towards the same goal—of that I am sure. But that does not mean that one has to lay down rules for every people. The point of the concept of cultural revolution is that man has to rise above the level of the capitalist reproduction process for the satisfaction of life's necessities. We cannot wait until we are sated with material goods. A level of basic needs has to be defined, and a standard of living may be achieved in underdeveloped countries that may be more rational than our own.

You are certainly right in saying that the socialist model of development and consumption should be other than the one prevalent in advanced capitalist countries. And you are also right that it would be very good for the people of Vietnam not to have to go through exactly the same process that the advanced capitalist countries have had to go through. But to conclude that underdeveloped countries can have a slow growth-rate—and, more important, that they can achieve a model of industrious, disciplined labour through such a cultural redivision of labour, before they have even had a capitalist division of labour—this is strictly what Marx would have called a utopia. It is to jump stages in order to create a sort of uniform world at one stroke out of a profoundly differentiated world. All historical experience speaks against this. It is like saying that the rich should give to the poor, in the sense that it is simply not a socially effective programme.

It is true that in my book I only developed one particular pattern, and it may be more appropriate for the situation in Western Europe. However, I am convinced that the GDR and Czechoslovakia are rich enough, and I always reject the argument put forward by Party comrades that a shortage of something or other in the GDR means that we must redouble our efforts to satisfy material needs in the old way. I fear that the logical consequence of your position is that the capitalist model will be given free rein in determining the pattern of development of these peoples.

Mao's point of departure was to ask whether communism can be built in more backward conditions than those of surrounding countries. That is still the great problem, and Mao was undoubtedly right to pose it in that way.

And yet, the Chinese are now talking about modernization and industrial development—which seems to confirm Marx's view that the development towards communism can only successfully take place on the basis of a high level of industrialization. This is the difference between Marxism and utopianism.

But if we don't go on making such efforts, the chances that mankind will perish become that much greater. People have to be prepared to re-think fundamentally their social structure and their needs. Think of what Moses was able to achieve.

It sounds as if you are making human will the driving force of history.

No. It isn't a question of pure human will. You can talk about economic interests on various planes. Historical materialism wouldn't be valid if the adoption of Christianity under the Roman Empire had not had a dimension of material interest that cut across the whole class structure. When a nation, or even mankind itself, faces the question of its own survival, then certain material interests recede into the background. The world's material resources, such as oil, coal or iron ore, are fast being depleted. Our civilization, with its established technology and structure of needs, cannot be maintained. I don't understand how one can refuse to face this.

That's a different question.

What I mean to say is that there are compelling material reasons for us to think, like Mao Tse-tung, in terms that might normally be considered utopian or voluntarist.

Can we pass to another broad question that is raised by what you said a moment ago. What seems to be lacking in your way of looking at capitalism in the West is any real awareness of the material resistance of the bourgeoisie as a class to socialism and social change generally. Similarly you tend to see the state as a large economic machine necessary for the reproduction of society, but not, in the classical Marxist sense, as an armed and repressive apparatus. You argue that today the prospect of ecological disaster provides the basis for a 'historic compromise'. But why do you imagine that the ruling class in the West will listen to appeals of this kind? After all, Marx himself rightly said in the mid-nineteenth century that communism would be a universal transformation from which even individual bourgeois would benefit. But why should the bourgeoisie heed such advice any more than in the past? There would seem no reason to change our view that socialism will come about only through revolutionary struggle, *not through a historic compromise with the ruling class.*

I think that Marxism, and especially Leninism, present a very narrow view of the state as a purely repressive force. In reality, it has acquired a large number of social functions whose statist nature and aspect of domination can be done away with, but which cannot themselves be suppressed. Moreover, at times when there is a mass readiness for a new society, it becomes much easier to neutralize the repressive apparatuses of the state.

But there will still be a real physical struggle. Just think of China or Vietnam, for instance.

Those were colonial-type situations, and what we are talking about is the developed capitalist countries. What was proven in Germany, I believe—and in Chile—is that the strategy of frontal assault is misconceived. The Spartakist Rising of 1919 showed that. What I describe as a historic compromise is not class collaboration but an attempt to strip the state of its role an an instrument of capitalist domination at all levels. This could be done if we had a real movement of the majority—not just in electoral terms but a real mass movement that swept through the whole of public opinion. It would then be possible to open a breach between the state as a capitalist apparatus and the state as a structure in which millions of working people are employed.

It is still not clear why you talk of a historic compromise.The position of the Italian Communist Party, for example, is quite clearly that the general situation in Italy is not ripe for socialism, and that a historic compromise is therefore necessary for a whole epoch. That seems very different from your point of view.

The PCI's conception of historic compromise does not seem to me to have been finally decided, but in any case the crucial question is that of reaching the Catholic masses under the influence of Christian Democracy. Berlinguer has drawn the conclusion from the experience of Chile that a frontal-assault strategy, even with 51 per cent of the population behind you, would fail because the international bourgeoisie could so easily disorganize industrial production and bring the country to a standstill. And when that point is reached, large sections of the population would turn against the revolution.

That argument could have been used in 1917. But the real point is: even if we accept Berlinguer's programme, how can it be reconciled with the programme of cultural revolution put forward in your book? On the one hand you have a very modest political strategy for the West—not so different from that of classical social democracy; on the other hand you have a tremendously radical social and economic programme. How can the two possibly be matched? Surely it is absurd to imagine that a Strauss or an Agnelli would be receptive to your ideas.

What you say is no doubt true of certain sections of capitalists. But even in America there are others who, faced with the atom bomb, have realized that the class struggle cannot be conducted at the same level as before. The dual threat of nuclear war and ecological disaster can even lead elements within the bourgeoisie to place the interests of survival above their class interests; and the range of such vital questions, which concern man as such, is growing ever broader.

Let me draw an analogy and try to imagine a Marxist at the time of Julius Caesar analysing the history of class struggles from the Gracchi through the Civil War down to the Spartacus Revolt. Sensing the crisis that hung over Roman civilization, he would have realized that the way out lay not in the old class divisions of slaves and freemen and so on but in existential demands that cut right across the existing class structures. Engels himself said that two things enabled Rome to recover—Germanic barbarism and Christianity. Applied to our own time, this means that the movement of regeneration will not be a proletarian movement or an anti-proletarian movement, but a movement of all classes. Again, it is not a question of class collaboration but of a compromise in the face of the crisis—atom bomb, nuclear power, ecological disaster—that threatens us all.

One simple response to your analogy is that Christianity, although a very impressive historical phenomenon, did not change the social and material structures—quite the contrary, it changed with them. Slavery continued, the empire continued, the Sermon on the Mount was never realized: it was an important superstructural change, but in no way did it determine the change from slavery to feudalism, any more than it did the change from feudalism to capitalism.

That is to put things rather too simply. Christianity alone was not responsible for feudalism, which then stood on the historical agenda. But in the Dark Ages the Benedictine slogan *ora et labora* made its own contribution to Italy's economic recovery. There is at least an interaction between ideological and material processes, so that, for example, Christianity's involvement with the poor led to an absence of discrimination against manual labour.

To start with, perhaps, but then everything changed.

As it became the ruling Church within the feudal system, you certainly found the normal class divisions within the monastery: some sat thinking in their cell, others worked in the garden, and so forth. The situation today is that material conditions make it possible for everybody to become an intellectual—in the first instance in the developed countries. If historical materialism is valid, then there must have been powerful material factors at work in the Middle Ages for an ideology to have expanded for four hundred years, determining the shape of a whole civilization. Similarly, I think that material factors today are furthering the kind of compromise that is forced upon us by the ecological crisis. Classical conflicts like 1789 were not so profound by comparison. The cultural revolution that we are all facing is comparable only with the transformation of man the nomadic hunter into man the agricultural settler.

But in that case, one would have thought that the social convulsions and the intensity of struggle will be incomparably greater than in the bourgeois revolution. If you take it seriously, the compromise analogous with Constantine's embracing of Christianity would be an announcement by President Carter that America will change the division of labour within the next ten years.

I see a great danger in persisting with the idea of a convulsive change in our society. Class distinctions become less significant in the face of the central challenge facing the world, and there is much that can be done together with the European or American bourgeoisie.

But it is only forty or fifty years since this European bourgeoisie gave rise to fascism.

It is much too simplistic to say that the European bourgeoisie gave rise to fascism, that its own culture pointed in that direction. The European bourgeoisie is sufficiently cultured for some of its elements to embrace the kind of alliance between labour and culture that the Italian Communist Party is advocating. In Eastern Europe, for example, it was often the case that large farmers became the best agricultural team-leaders after the war. Today there is a division between the truly parasitic, playboy-like bourgeois elements and others who are no longer concerned with the ownership of gold plates and so forth. They are, to be sure, wedded to their role in authoritarian command structures, but that is a problem which will itself only gradually be resolved through a process of cultural revolution. So long as there is a sufficiently strong mass movement, the bourgeoisie can be forced to regard the military option as an irrational course. I therefore agree with the Greens' idea that non-violent resistance has greater prospects of bringing about the necessary change: non-violence is a line followed only by those who are active supporters of a new world. To attempt a second Chile would be the worst thing we could do.

Everything you have been saying seems a long way from The Alternative. *There you advance a programme of change to a communist society in which the division of labour is abolished and so on. What you are now talking about is an ecological programme.*

Maybe there has been a shift of emphasis in my thinking, but the two questions are not that far apart. I believe that the ecological crisis will bring about the end of capitalism, and that is why I have associated myself with the Greens in West Germany.

But there are many people among the Greens who have nothing whatever to do with socialism.

Yes, you would be surprised. I gave a speech in Karlsruhe not long ago, pointing out that the ecological crisis cannot be solved without putting an end to the arms race between East and West, without a new economic order between North and South, without social justice, human emancipation and so forth. People said to me that I was trying to foist a socialist programme on the Greens, but then I told them to read the draft programme for the Green Congress in Saarbrücken. All these points are contained in it, although not everyone would interpret them in the same way.

If the vanguard is itself divided, what hope is there of reaching the goal?

My main task in West Germany, as I see it, is to help to unite the forces of socialism with those of the ecologists. The socialists have been too bound by their own historical traditions and concepts to bring about this union. They have not been prepared to realize how serious those people are who say that they want nothing to do with capitalism or fascism on the one hand, or with so-called communism on the other. Eventually a new bloc will emerge and bring unity on the basis of an anti-capitalist economy, human emancipation and a solution to the ecological crisis.

At one point when I was working on my book in the GDR, I become aware that these various components somehow fitted together, but I couldn't yet see their precise mode of articulation. I want to devote myself to this question in the future.

Do you find the same sort of basis for an ecological movement in the GDR?

As I have said elsewhere in connection with Italy, my hopes for positive developments in the GDR rest to a large extent with progressive elements in the Party, for that is where most of the active potential lies. The ecological question is therefore intimately bound up with the more general movement for reform.

Do you think that the Greens can play the role of what you call a Communist League?

The word 'communist' can be confusing—some people think of Stalinism, others of what could be called democratic communism, others again, perhaps, of what Marx imagined communism to be. But although there is a risk that I might be misunderstood in West Germany, I would maintain that the ecological movement, in its true complexity, ultimately conforms to the communist perspective.

Part Two

Part Two

5
In the Bundesrepublik

You have been living in West Germany for two years or so now. Let us open this second part of our discussion by asking what impressions you have of life in the West, especially what has surprised you.

That's difficult to say off the cuff. I think that what surprised me most, right from the beginning, was how little actually did surprise me. I was more or less prepared for a lot of the things I found, so that the experiences themselves only confirmed, in concrete terms, what I had expected. The fact that the GDR and West Germany lie side by side probably had something to do with this, together with the relative continuity of the German historical process. In any case, I am not a man to be greatly dependent on the details of my physical environment. Automatic doors and other such symbols of the affluent society only struck me in the first few days, and the big department stores never made much impression on me. Nor had those on Alexanderplatz back in East Berlin, come to that: I always preferred to buy books and gramophone records in other places.

One thing I did find very surprising was the psychological defeatism that had penetrated the West German Left since 1967–68, when so many had believed that the kingdom of heaven was at hand. The experience of broken promises deeply disillusioned the activists of '68 and convinced them that there was no way forward. Indeed, in a personalization of failure that I found quite impermissible, many would get angry when you tried to tell them that certain things could still be done. The depressing history of Germany since the First World War naturally contributed to this sense of historical pessimism and made many cling to the Social Democrats as the last hope against a repressive regime of the Right. Only very recently, with the development of the Alternative List in Berlin, have there been some signs of a change of direction.

There is in the West, particularly in Britain and the United States, a high degree of cultural disintegration at certain levels of society. The media, for example, systematically exploit themes of violence, and these are written into the culture of large sections of the youth. In Eastern Europe one probably does not find this, because there the media are very strictly controlled.

I don't think that controls are the main reason for the difference. I didn't watch much television when I was in the GDR, but it was clear that this process of disintegration was far more advanced in the West, even if one didn't want to idealize conditions in the East. I could see this in my own son, who is always inclined to defend the GDR, not unthinkingly or because he has forgotten what there is to criticize but because he can see with his own eyes that everyday life for young people is not preferable in the Federal Republic. The common denominator is what I would call instability—the instability that results from the lack of a firm system of values. Maybe this is less pronounced in the East, but basically the same processes of industrialization are at work on both sides, as, ultimately, are the same processes of cultural development and the same destructive tendencies. The differences lie above all in the realm of politics, in the relations of power and so on.

Today, the individualism of the civilization of the West is combined with the declining significance of individual actions—a development that seems to me more crucial than the feeling of insignificance which the individual experiences in relation to the all-embracing power of the state. Inner values are being defined in terms of mass external patterns and conditions which can no longer be integrated at the level of the individual. In this sense the personality is disintegrating more rapidly in the West than in the East.

In the GDR, where there was no public forum for discussion of the issues that concerned you, you had to develop your ideas in relative isolation. What is your opinion of the standard of discussion that takes place in the forum available in the West?

My answer may sound impertinent, but I shall say it nonetheless. On the one hand there are a host of valuable detailed analyses of cultural factors based upon solid empirical research. On the other hand, when it comes to more strictly theoretical analysis, everything seems to take place at a highly rarefied meta-level of generalization that is incapable of addressing the burning problems of our time. There is a mass of hair-splitting and an overriding fear of being caught out or falling into some illusion. I can pick up the odd point here and there from these writings, but in the main I find them quite unproductive. Contemporary left-wing ideology seems incapable of putting forward a constructive plan for the future. As far as West Germany is concerned, this is due in particular to the fact that Germany lacks the historical continuity of thought that one finds, for example, in France, where many different currents survived intact and where Marxism did not simply disappear from the scene. In Germany almost an entire generation was left without a background of Marxist theory. One result of this was that the best of German exile literature in the 1930s and 1940s was written in the tradition of bourgeois literature.

Was that true of Brecht?

In the broadest sense, yes. Perhaps 'bourgeois literature' is not the best term, but his subject-matter is certainly bourgeois life as a whole. *Galileo*, for instance—a key work of his exile years—is concerned with the problem of bourgeois culture and bourgeois science, not just reducing them to class terms but relating them to the entire epoch. Even Marxist writers like Heinrich Mann and Feuchtwanger drew their subject-matter from the political and cultural world of the bourgeoisie.

Between 1930 and 1960 we had no real Marxism in Germany, so that the Left had to recover its experience of Marxism by going back to the original texts. Marx and the Frankfurt School are so far apart, and the later appearance of Maoism somehow made the whole thing still less organic. For those who made the deepest analysis, the crucial element was probably the experience of the Frankfurt School:

namely, that Germany's lack of a democratic past had left a kind of resentment towards the historical reality of the German situation, and that this provided a weak position from which to launch a programme of action. Not long after I arrived in the West, I was given a copy of a thousand-page volume edited by Habermas, *The Intellectual Situation of the Age*. It was written with great critical acumen, but it continually drew defeatist conclusions.

How would you generally view the work of Habermas, which is now beginning to have some resonance outside West Germany?

I have not yet fully absorbed his work, but it seems to me to represent the end of a particular line of thought. Like a number of others, he is taking the pulse of capitalist society, so to speak, and trying to describe ever more accurately what is going on. Yet this seems to lead him into a historical impasse, with the result that it is the scientifically less substantial figures of Marcuse and Erich Fromm who seem to offer the only interesting and fruitful possibilities.

Let us turn to the present political situation in West Germany. You have been actively engaged with the Green movement since your arrival in the West. How do you assess its prospects?

Before I go into that, I would like to stress that the 'Green' movement should be understood in rather broad terms. The name itself is misleading, in that it conjures up images of trees, nature and so on, whereas in fact it is a broad ideological movement that reaches beyond the mechanisms of bourgeois society. Not that it ignores the existing reality, but it does not believe that Western industrial society can offer a solution to our problems. It combines a number of trends that are present in all classes of society and all political groups, creating a new field of interest in the sense that one talks of a magnetic field. It is difficult to absorb this into the existing party political system, and so the ecology movement has in fact turned into an alternative type of party. I first saw for myself how people came from all different quarters to unite in the movement, when I attended the Church Congress in Hamburg in 1979, where there were Catholics, Protestants, left-wing Social Democrats and other left groupings, the Young Liberals of the Free Democratic Party, and many others.

Why is it only Germany, of the major capitalist countries, that has so far produced an ecology party of any importance?

I'm not sure that that is the right way to put it. In Holland, for instance, the ecology movement is much stronger than in Germany, so there is no need for a political party. Besides, it embraces trends like the peace movement, the third-world movement and the revival of basic Christianity in the Churches, so that we really need a better name than 'ecology movement'. One might ask why it has first come to the fore in the countries stretching from Scandinavia down to Austria and Switzerland. In Italy, by contrast, such issues are over-shadowed by the struggle that is going on between the radical Left and the Communist Party. When I was in Bologna, I saw a young comrade carrying a placard on which was painted a tombstone with a large black cross and the inscription: 'Berlinguer—My Love'. This symbolizes the level of the argument, though there are signs that the ecology movement is beginning to make an impression there too. Still, it is an interesting fact that most countries where ecological interests are really on the rise are traditionally Protestant. The time may also be ripe for such a development in England, although the fact of Britain's early industrialization and imperial past may tend to hold it back.

Part of the reason for its relative weakness in England may be that the highly capitalized agriculture deprives it of a rural social base.

Perhaps. The century-old confrontation between Conservative and Labour is probably also responsible: people think first in party-political terms and pay relatively little attention to new issues. It is possible that the strong anti-nuclear movement in Britain will provide a basis.

How far is it the case in West Germany that the Green movement, in its more structured political aspect, has become the dominant force on the Left? Or would you not accept that way of posing the question?

The traditional Left has been pushed further and further from the centre of the stage and can now barely keep its head above water—you can see that from the struggle for survival of their newspaper in Berlin. The SPD groupings which support disarmament and so on have no really long-term vision of their own, and the far Left is now taking its bearings from the Greens. Even the West German Communist Party, although clearly not in any hurry, has expressed its willingness to discuss the issues with the others. That is quite a contrast to the way *Neues Deutschland* paints the Alternatives as a capitalist fifth column.

Would you say that there are significant regional variations within the West German ecology movement?

In most northern districts the driving force comes from the Left, whereas in Bavaria and Baden-Württemberg, and also in Lower Saxony, the emphasis lies more on the environmental side, where one also finds conservative elements from the older generation. In places like Berlin and Frankfurt these older people are put off by the noisiness and violence of young left-wing demonstrators.

Many people are being drawn to the Green movement who would never formerly have committed themselves to a political party. They don't necessarily become members but they turn up at meetings which discuss particular issues. You find teachers among them, for example, including divinity teachers, both Protestant and Catholic, and others who find historical relevance in one or other of the lines of argument put forward. This is why it is better to leave the organizational structure fairly loose than to try to direct policy from the centre, because then ideological differences would show up which hinder the progress of the movement. The unity in the movement is a unity of long-term aims, and the members are more or less clear about the way things are moving. They are all in favour of unilateral nuclear disarmament, for instance, and not of the line taken by the German Communist Party. There are good reasons for thinking that an increasing number of people will come round to this view of things.

How do you see recent developments inside the SPD itself? It would seem that there has been a big change in the last two years, with the growth of a new opposition.

It is my opinion that German Social Democracy, in the form it has existed for the last hundred and twenty years, is facing its ultimate crisis. For although the struggle with the capitalist class for a higher standard of living is still a real issue, it is no longer the principal area of concern. Hitherto the SPD has sought to extract the greatest possible benefits from the industrial system for the lower classes—education, the welfare state and so on. This naturally requires continual growth and rising profits, whereas growth and profits are in fact falling and the cost of armaments and of the ever-swelling bureaucracy is eating deeper into our resources. Perhaps the most important aspect of this is that it is virtually impossible for the SPD to mobilize the support of the Left, or even to neutralize its influence. Both these things still seemed possible back in 1968, when the situation was formulated in the classical Marxist terms of the working-class struggle, and when the SPD was still constituted as the party of the working class. But the ecology movement has shown that the crucial task now is to break with the traditional processes of industrial society, and that the working class forms a second industrial class alongside the bourgeoisie. The way we put it is: How can the total process of reproduction be slowed down? And when you look at it in this light, the political ethos and all the political assumptions of the SPD are called into question.

The SPD Premier of Hesse—to take but one example—is determined to build a new runway for Frankfurt airport, and to press on with the construction of nuclear reactors, arguing that all this creates jobs, helps the workers and so forth. The Alternative Movement contests this whole approach and whole philosophy, but no longer in the manner of the old Young Socialist appeals to the tradition of Otto Bauer or the Erfurt Programme. Some of the old phrases still crop up here and there, but that line of thought has lost its impetus and its inner consistency.

Is it not true that, as far as the new opposition within the SPD is concerned, the arms race is a more central issue than questions of

I would put it the other way round: the ecological problem comes first and the arms race is then fitted into the picture. To be sure, the arms question engages the energies of the most important figures on the parliamentary Left, such as Brandt and Egon Bahr, although the central figure in this opposition within the SPD is Erhard Eppler. All three are committed to disarmament, and of course I approve of this; but the point I want to make is that the peace movement has its best chances of success when it is ultimately linked to the ecology movement. After all, the arms race ultimately rests upon the mechanisms of competition and economic growth, with which it is half-consciously connected. Although nuclear bombs may well be more of a threat than nuclear power-stations, it is always the same people within the SPD rank-and-file who are active on struggles concerning disarmament, aid to Third World countries, or the halting of nuclear energy programmes.

How, then, do you see the situation developing in the SPD?

The first thing I would say is that the electoral ground of the SPD is slipping away both to the Right and to the Greens. In fact, since it is becoming too narrow to form a basis for remaining in power, Vogel, the moderate SPD leader in Berlin, launched his electoral campaign with a promise to preserve law and order more efficiently, so as to prevent the Christian Democrats from capitalizing on social disturbances in the city. The SPD can no longer persuade the Left—as Berlin and Frankfurt have proven—to vote for the lesser of two evils, and the result in both cases was a local election victory for the CDU. Nor were the two CDU leaders in these cases extremists, like Franz-Josef Strauss in Bavaria. The argument that the Left should automatically vote SPD no longer carried any conviction for that layer which switched its allegiance to the Alternatives. Even if the Alternatives had made an alliance with the SPD, they could not have gained control of Berlin, because the CDU had between 47 and 48 per cent of the seats, whereas the SPD and the Alternatives combined had only some 45 per cent. The same was true in Frankfurt.

What we are seeing is a tendency towards conservatism in all groups and classes in society. People want to leave things as they are, and so they accept that those who disturb the peace should be effectively dealt with. It is not an aggressive conservatism of the Strauss type but a moderate position reflecting people's sense of insecurity and their instinctive rejection of actions like squatting. The fact is that West Germany has a Helmut Schmidt Party. From the point of view of mentality and ideology Chancellor Schmidt represents the CDU as well as the SPD and the FDP. He is far better than his party, and that is one of the reasons why this conservative bloc exists. He has the support of the right wing of the FDP, of Foreign Minister Genscher, of course, and also of the more traditionally minded members of the SPD, including the skilled workers. This makes up the conservative centre, as distinct from the conservative Right, who voted for people like Strauss in order to keep the Social Democrats out. In fact, only some fifteen per cent of those prepared to vote for a Schmidt–Vogel 'law-and-order' policy would support a genuinely authoritarian course.

After the Berlin local elections in 1980, when the CDU came to power, left-wing members of the SPD carried out an analysis which showed that potential support for the SPD was disintegrating. The Alternative List got between seven and eight per cent of the vote, but among intellectuals their share was some twenty per cent—which means that many of those on the Marxist Left whom the SPD had tried to keep within its ranks had turned to the Alternatives in search of quite different policies. The trade unions, on the other hand, are largely behind Chancellor Schmidt, seeing that as the only way of protecting jobs and various past gains.

Do you think that the Schmidt government might be obliged to abandon its NATO rearmament plans in the next two years?

That would require a complete shift away from the SPD's pro-NATO policy, towards a position of neutrality. The United States obviously has a vested interest in deploying these nuclear missiles in NATO countries, because it establishes the long-term dependence of Europe, especially of West Germany. However, Schmidt could only be forced to change his policies—or to resign—if the peace movement gained the support of, let us say, sixty or seventy per cent of the population. There is, of course, a special problem in putting our ideas across. If we demonstrate in some small town or other in order to point out that the nearby missile site would certainly be a target for Russian rockets in the event of war, the inhabitants are still more afraid of the dramatic and sometimes violent methods of the young demonstrators than they are of the Russian rockets. We have to realize that in the long term we can only get people on our side by argument, not by hysterics and 'direct action'. It is a psychological matter. People must be convinced that it is not Russian missiles that are threatening their homes but their own government's policies which are increasing the likelihood of war. Young people in the peace movement are, I think, already becoming more aware of the need for a rational approach, and occasions like the Council of Churches meeting in Hamburg that I mentioned offer the best chance—a militant but non-violent course.

In addition to this long-term strategic aspect, there is the matter of how to bring pressure to bear on the SPD itself, because we need a great number of political activists, and many of these are to be found in the ranks of the SPD. Even people like Vogel in Berlin seem to have grasped the nature of the politico-psychological constellation and to be seeking a mediation between the positions of Schmidt and Eppler. But I can only repeat: the SPD has no chance of survival if it does not undergo a change at least as radical as that which it experienced after 1945.

How are relations between the SPD Left and the Green or Alternative movement?

There's no straightforward answer to that question. Until the beginning of 1981, the SPD had dealt with the Green challenge by trying to ignore it. But since then, under Willi Brandt's influence, there has been a move to engage in genuine dialogue with us. In Darmstadt, for instance, the town council is run by the SPD in collaboration with the Greens, and in Kassel too, I believe. Where both are in opposition, as in Berlin and Frankfurt, they inevitably confer with each other, because the SPD sees the constructive contribution we can make, while realizing that it has been steadily losing ground to the Right and the Left.

As soon as we discuss ideological matters, the question of party allegiance fades into the background and we in the Green Movement have no difficulty in communicating with the SPD Left. In mass demonstrations, however, the SPD is sometimes the target of a vocal opposition that does not distinguish between Horst Ehmke, for example, who defends the policy of rearmament, and the Young Socialists, who oppose it. Even I have found myself shouted down for pleading for calm discussion instead of a mere chanting of slogans. There are also those among the Alternatives who don't believe in elections at all. If we carried this division to its limits, it would mean splitting the SPD, with the left wing joining the Alternatives. But I don't see that as the best solution, because it would restrict our range of possibilities if we were to present a definitive socialist programme to the country.

One might reply that this is a symptom of the kind of defeatism you've been discussing: namely, that explicit references to socialism restrict your capacity to win people over.

No, you're talking about two different things. The defeatism I described earlier is the virtually inevitable consequence of a traditional conception of socialism. For experience shows that any policies based on that position seem doomed to failure. My own position is not only that the questions traditionally posed by the Left will restrict our room for manoeuvre, but that they are anyway not the questions which matter most. Our task must be to put the principal questions in the forefront, just as they stand, as individual issues, not as a complete programme.

Can we now turn to another matter on which it would be interesting to hear your views? In your essay on exterminism you argue that in fighting against the prospect of nuclear war, we must oppose not only nuclear power as such but also the whole of modern industry. But although many people sense the threat of nuclear war or the danger of nuclear power stations, as an uncontrolled form of technology, there are far fewer who will accept that electricity generators or coalmining imperil the human species. By linking the two, are you not restricting the appeal of the peace movement to a relatively narrow group of convinced radical ecologists?

I can see the point of your question as far as Britain is concerned, and I certainly don't want to imply that my own way of looking at things is the only way I will accept. My starting-point is the situation in the Bundesrepublik, where I believe that the ecology movement adds to the potential influence of the peace movement. Without this broad framework for our activity, I am convinced that we shall never put an end to the arms race, whatever little successes we may have with Cruise and Pershing or other specific issues.

When I was in Frankfurt, Daniel Cohn-Bendit made a remark at a meeting which corresponded exactly with my own attitude. If half the population of Germany had their own little house with an oil central-heating tank in their cellar, he said, they could be persuaded, in the event of an oil crisis, that a task force should be sent to the Persian Gulf. That is to say, militarism is a natural consequence of the dependence on raw materials of our over-worked production system. Without a basic change in our civilization, our productive forces and so on, there is no hope of avoiding catastrophe in the long run. Moreover, such a change will alter human behaviour and human culture in general, which is at present conditioned by the form of technology in our societies.

Nor must we forget that nuclear weapons are proliferating, that in important Third World countries a Hitler-type figure may resort to violence in order to distract attention from his failure to deal with hunger, poverty and other internal pressures. Since all the North–South conferences offer no prospect of reconciling the interests of the industrialized nations—the USA, Japan, Europe and, secondarily, the heartlands of the Eastern bloc—with those of the underdeveloped countries, there will have to be a fundamental change in our own aggressive industrial system.

Your argument has an inner logic, but might it not be tactically unwise to pursue it in so comprehensive and binding a form at the present time? You say that, in the long run, the fate of one particular weapons system is not all that important. But Sweden, for instance, has refused to have nuclear weapons on its soil or to abandon its bloc-free position, yet it remains a highly industrialized country with an advanced system of nuclear energy.

I consider it an illusion to believe that in countries like West Germany, France and Britain, which are part and parcel of the Cold War situation, the problem can be solved by a single-issue campaign. It has to be directed at the Cold War mentality and the Cold War complex as a whole. How could it be otherwise? If you were to hold a referendum in Britain on the single issue of whether to abandon rearmament and the principle of nuclear defence, you wouldn't get a majority, because people are not psychologically prepared for such a step. It has to be part of a deeper and fuller awareness.

If you are saying that the root of the problem lies in the Cold War structures of the confrontation between the United States and the Soviet Union, then perhaps we will find ourselves in agreement. But you seem to have shifted the basis of your argument, which was that our industrial system is the real problem to be attacked. And you haven't answered the point about Sweden.

I don't consider Sweden an argument. Different nations occupy different positons vis-à-vis the political centre of the industrialized capitalist system—some are further from the centre than others, for geographical and historical reasons, and can avoid some of its more extreme manifestations. But the system remains one system, and through its aggressive character it has forced the whole world to follow the same sink-or-swim path. Sweden may not be directly involved in the Cold War confrontation, but it is caught up in the process like any other country. Even the Russian Revolution should be understood by reference to a centuries-old struggle of the old ruling class to catch up with the West—to patch up the system somehow or other in order to avoid total collapse. For the majority of mankind there is a more drastic dilemma than that which faced Russia in 1917, because if the economic gulf between North and South continues to widen, and if we fail to change the type of reproduction in the advanced capitalist countries, then I do not see how war can be prevented.

If we look historically at the different phases of capitalist develop-

ment, it is not the case that there has been a constant level of militarism, a universal level of militarism. You seem to adopt a maximalist position that the threat of nuclear war can only be eliminated if industry is itself removed from the picture. But surely there are certain common interests of survival that even militarists share.

We must distinguish between the possibility of preventing, or at least delaying, a catastrophe and the need to extricate ourselves from the frightening situation as a whole. When you look at the amount of raw materials that our society uses up; when you think of the steps we take to avoid the danger of losing our Middle East oil supplies; and when you look at the way in which the developing countries are placed on the treadmill of the arms race—then you can see how vital it is to go to the heart of the matter. Our protests in Europe against nuclear weapons have not the slightest effect on the Third World arms build-up—not the slightest effect. If a political movement is to have a chance of success, it must have an overall historical conception of its aim. An historical example of what I mean would be the Roman Empire. Without the *limes* and the legions the Empire would be unthinkable. It might have been possible to prevent a particular legion from being recruited in the year 250, say, but the only result would have been that it was recruited a couple of years later in some other place. It was the only means of defending the metropolis, and in time the population came to agree that it was.

What you say is very persuasive on one level, but at the same time the Cold War is surely, in essence, a conflict between two different social and political systems.

The situation in which we set about overcoming the conditions created by the Cold War today is quite different from that in which the Cold War first arose. When we look at the situation in Europe today, with its clearly demarcated areas of political and military interest, we could conclude that the threat of a third world war is non-existent. But whenever there is a challenge to the political hegemony in Eastern Europe, the whole war machine goes into action. The confrontation between America and the Soviet Union has a world-wide dimension, and any event that happens—in El Salvador, Angola,

Iran—raises the question of whether it helps the Americans or the Russians. A revolution in Saudi Arabia, for example, might trigger off a world war, and this broader reality is more important than the specific political origins of the Cold War. For me the Cold War is connected with the confrontation between the capitalist world and the non-capitalist world, and the international conflict of 1917 has its parallel today in the North–South conflict. The ruling classes in capitalist states are more and more adopting a mentality like that of the Israelis or the South African whites. This is true above all of the Reagan administration—and it is not just a product of anti-Sovietism, because Reagan's more intelligent advisers cannot possibly believe all that talk about the Soviet Union being the fount of world revolution.

Again I would take the analogy of ancient Rome, where unrest in the towns was feared in the event that the legions would be unable to guarantee safe passage for grain-ships through the Mediterranean. In such situations one sees potential enemies everywhere, threatening the lines of communication. One senses today that the source of the problem lies in one's backyard, but one looks around for some general explanation and justification in the activity of hostile forces in the outside world. A general feeling of insecurity sets in, and we return to the Cold War mentality in a far more central, all-embracing way than after the end of the Second World War. For today the crisis in our industrial system has taken on far greater proportions, and this is ultimately what is responsible for the growing militarization. The contradictions inherent in our industrial cities are functions of a broader play of forces with which we are becoming less and less able to cope.

In your article on the arms race and exterminism, you also make a very tight equation between nuclear arms, nuclear power and the arms industry, in fact, capitalist industrialization of any sort. Yet at the end of the article you advocate a defence plan for West Germany which would involve a considerable array of armaments. Do you not see a contradiction here?

I only touch on this in my article, and anyway it isn't presented as the solution to everything. My final argument, indeed, is that even the so-called alternative defence policy ultimately forms part of the exterminist context. It is a response at the level of practical politics, so to speak, but in the end we must develop a radical eco-pacifist alternative, of the kind that certain circles in the Protestant Church represent. However, since there is a general obsession for defence of one kind or another, I simply speculated that it might be possible to develop an indisputably defensive system with weapons demonstrably incapable of launching an attack. The only damage they could cause would then be to enemy territory over which they had been sent up to ward off a suspected attack. If discussions along these lines were possible, they might help to defuse the situation and gain time. They might at least prevent further escalation, which is our greatest fear.

How would you describe the difference between your long-term eco-pacifist position and that of traditional pacifism, as far as the arms race is concerned?

The difference lies precisely in the central point we have been discussing. Traditional pacifism belongs in the context of liberalism, often Christian liberalism, and is therefore inseparable from the industrialist vision of putting the products of the system to better and more humane use. 'Lay down your arms!' was the old slogan. But since rearmament is part and parcel of the system, the German Social Democrats in the early twentieth century hesitated to oppose it. As I see the situation today, this militarism goes deeper than Marx described it in *Das Kapital*, so that our opposition to it must also go deeper. It is no accident that European civilization first led to capitalism and to the aggressive policies bound up with it. It is all historically conditioned, and I wonder whether man's whole development since the Renaissance has, in this respect, not been an aberration. We ought at least to face up to the question, and this is at the back of my mind when I say that we must break with our present industrial system. At the very least, it does not seem possible to argue that our problems will be resolved through the process of industrialization.

To see the development of industry as an aberration has nothing to do with Marx's view of historical evolution. He may have been wrong, of course, but he saw industrial capitalism not as an accident but as an inevitable and progressive development from feudalism, given the existing level of the productive forces.

You say 'inevitable development'. Marx took it for granted that inevitable development was to be equated with inevitable progress— but this is far from proven. If we look at biological evolution, we see that the development of a species is not a linear upward movement: a species can die, the evolutionary process can take a wrong turning. Every historical biologist will tell you that one has to fear for the survival of a successful species or genus that disturbs the balance of the other species among which it lives. There is no biological analogy to the power and success of homo sapiens. Marx never asked whether the earth might have finite limits, because in his time there were no limits in sight. But when we look at the rising world population, and cannot find a square inch of land that has not been dug up and cultivated or built on, it is clear that our material consumption and our squandering of energy and other resources cannot go in the same way.

Your implicit rejection of historical materialism remains, though.

I don't follow this. It is no part of historical materialism that one has to believe in unbounded progress. It just happens to share this whole confidence in Man, the spirit of optimism, that has characterized Europe since the Renaissance.

We should distinguish between the decay of a social system that is not replaced in time by a higher form of society—the case of capitalism today—and the original development of capitalism as a progressive form in relation to feudalism. If you say that the appearance of capitalism was a historical aberration, you must show what other form of development could have taken place at that time.

Your argument assumes that the nature and structure of the

contradictions of the feudal system constitute everything that needs
to be brought into discussion of subsequent developments. But
capitalism is the first social system in which man's relative independence of natural conditions has gone so far that he has almost
forgotten they exist. Now that social and economic contradictions
have assumed such a dominant role, we are fighting out our struggles
heedless of whether we destroy the biosphere on which our whole life
depends. Our excessive use of natural resources will take far too long
to correct, and what we use up now is at the expense of generations
to come.

*I would just like to recall a typical passage from your 'resumé of
premisses' in Part Two of* The Alternative. *You argue on page 128
that 'primarily, the state was the institution of civilization, of the
original formation of the different social bodies'. You make it clear
that this represented a historical progress, despite the conflict between special interests and general functions. 'How far the overall
relationship was justified,' you continue, 'can be precisely measured
by the historical gulf that today lies between the exploited industrial
workers and engineers of the rich countries, and—let us say—the
"freemen" in the Indian tribes of Latin America... The state as task-
master of society in its technical and social modernization—this
fundamental model can be found time and again since 1917,
wherever precapitalist countries or their decisive minorities have
organized themselves for active entry into the twentieth century. If
from this standpoint the Soviet Union is identical not only with
China, but also with Burma, Algeria or Guinea, and not only with
Guinea, but recently also with Peru or Zaire, and not only Zaire but
even Iran, where a Shah stemming from an era before classical antiquity is conducting his own "white revolution"—this only underlines
the fundamental value of the state in this context.' Now, this position does not really seem compatible with what you have been saying
today.*

Although the basic point remains true, the passage which you have
quoted comes from a section that I had neither time nor opportunity
to revise, and it may well be that my emphasis has changed since

then. In a speech I gave in Caracas, I made it clear that I had changed my position on the inevitability of industrialization for all the peoples of the world. In *The Alternative* the context was the narrower one of Eastern Europe, where the broader issues did not present themselves as insistently as they do when one considers the situation in the world as a whole. Chapter Ten concerns itself with some of these matters, but it is certainly true that I then saw industrialization as an inevitable path for the Soviet Union and as the necessary presupposition for the development of a communist society.

Somewhere in the fourth chapter of *The Alternative* I make the point that a communist society is not conceivable on a lower level than that dictated by the most advanced capitalist countries. I wasn't quite sure about this after I had finished the final section of the book, but I have since come to the view that it is quite simply impossible to put this formula into effect: that if all the countries of the world first have to reach this general level of development, then no progress will be possible because of the earth's finite resources. It was in the mid-seventies that I eventually became aware of these limits of nature. I was then still in the GDR, where pollution was at its height before the cleaning of the River Saale and other such measures. But since, at that time, I had no access to figures on the world situation, I couldn't yet see that it was impossible to think in terms of an expanding industrial system for everyone.

Can you then explain precisely what your programme of 'industrial disarmament' will involve. Are you going to prevent societies from having electricity, or modern means of communication, or the internal combustion engine and so on?

This is too simplistic a way of putting it. The things you mention only exist in the context of industrial society, and none of them can simply be extirpated from it. The real problem is that capitalist society appears to be the only large-scale civilization in which Marx's thesis of the decisive role of the economic forces of production applies in the literal terms in which it is formulated—the economic sphere as that which has subordinated all other spheres of life to itself. This is the essential meaning today of the concept of alienation.

It is still not clear what meaning you attach to the concept of 'industrial disarmament', or how you think it can be put across to the people at large.

My experience in the Bundesrepublik has convinced me that there would have been no ecology movement at all if people had first stopped to ask the question you are asking now. Nobody has yet given a precise answer, and yet the movement *has* come into existence. It is in general wrong to believe that social change can only be achieved if people have first been given a scientific explanation of what precisely can be done. The revolutionaries in Russia in 1917 wanted, in ideological terms, to do quite different things from those they actually did.

The masses wanted peace, land and bread, and that is more or less what they got.

Yes. But land and bread were for the Bolsheviks only means to an end—ways of gaining power in order to carry out their programme.

Bread and land were concrete goals that the people could understand, whereas you are asking us to make a leap in the dark. You say that our existing civilization is doomed but not what is to take its place.

I don't think this reflects a very thorough understanding of the Russian Revolution, or of any of the great revolutions. What did land, or peace, mean in Russia at that time? The Revolution happened not merely because of the general contradictions in the backward society of the time but because the people wanted to see an end to the war. Peace meant simply: no war—hence, to escape from the hardships, abuse etc. that the existing system had produced. The same applied to the question of land, to the misery of the peasant's lot.

That we have an ecology movement at all is due to the presence of a sufficiently strong feeling in a sufficiently large number of people; and if my prognosis of the disaster facing mankind has any rational basis to it, we shall find more and more people taking action to prevent it, especially in Western industrial nations. There will, in fact, be a classic revolutionary situation: those at the top cannot go on as before, and those below are no longer prepared to go on as before. This is how things stand now in the confrontation between the municipal authorities and the squatters in Berlin.

We often tend to reduce all the problems of resources to a socioeconomic level, arguing that capitalist reproduction alone accounts for the fact that much of mankind is not properly fed. And yet, it is becoming ever more difficult to envisage a solution. The more coal that is extracted, for example, the deeper we have to dig beneath the earth's surface and the more expensive the coal becomes. The choice, as I see it, is between the more or less peaceful dismantling of the huge structures we have built, and the collapse of the whole system, with even more disastrous consequences for future generations than for ourselves.

We seem completely to miscalculate the time factor when we discuss these matters. It has taken only two hundred years to reach the present situation. Just imagine what will happen if we try to do no more than reproduce the present standard of living in the developed countries for the whole of the present population of the world. All experience shows that those who have less want to have the same as others, and essentially in the same form because it is the only one they can conceive. The only solution is to break out of what historical materialism has always described as a natural-historical process.

The moves that have so far been made to change the course of our development do not seem to go to the heart of the problem—the Lucas Aerospace experiment, for example. The end result always seems to be: we want to go on producing in the same way, only we'll produce more useful things. The question of changing the reproduction process itself is never raised. People say: I'm a bricklayer, or a draughtsman, or an engineer, as if this were a natural form of existence rather than the expression of a given set of historical circumstances. It is as if men at an earlier stage had said: we are hunters and want to remain hunters, instead of passing on to agriculture. The real task now is to return to the question of the needs, interests and exigencies that stem from man's nature, independently of any particular historical situation.

Who is going to define these needs?

People will have to reach some kind of consensus about, for example, the number of cars that are necessary. But my basic point is that the Hegelian positivism taken over by Marxism, with its view that every product of necessary historical development is definitively written into our system of values, goes too far beyond the real structure of human need. If we look at the problem from the other end, as it were, the young Marx already saw that production had gained the upper hand in the dialectic of population and need, and we have to ask ourselves whether this relationship can be, and must be, reversed. In a sense this is what Marx himself had in mind when he talked about 'establishing the supremacy of living labour over dead labour'. Even if the lords of capitalism were really in control of things in the past—and there are good reasons for doubting this—there is today no one who can be held subjectively responsible, no class whose mere removal would break the vicious circle. We must ask how the 'surplus consciousness' which is not absorbed in the reproduction process can be mobilized and given primacy over material consciousness. My own view is that there can be no solution as long as this surplus consciousness is made the dependent quantity. But the position into which we are forced is not, 'historical materialism is false' but 'the leap into the realm of freedom must be possible even if the logic of the material process does not produce it'.

I would like to make two points in connection with this. The first is that the great revolutions were not the direct product simply of an overarching class contradiction, but stemmed from a general crisis in the culture of the time which brought great pressure to bear on the individual's human dignity and essence. We can see today that the capitalist system itself is beginning to force people to face up to this in the big cities. The ecological crisis means, among other things, that questions are coming onto the agenda which were already there before the first class society took shape. This is the primary source for the mobilization of psychological counter-forces.

Secondly, we must be prepared to utilize the historically tried means of mobilizing, focusing and reinforcing this surplus consciousness, so that the whole field which is scattered and atomized by the ruling structures may be drawn together. Nor can we do without that social and psychological experience which, in times of cultural revolution, has always been associated with religious mobilization. The problem is, of course, that religion is too rigidly defined in terms of the existing Churches, rather than the original experiences of Jesus Christ, Buddha and Lao Tse, or the millennial movements that did not succumb to a hierarchical order. Although we cannot jettison the whole Enlightenment tradition, a medieval mystic like Meister Eckhart also has a contribution to make, in that he poses God not as a transcendent power but as dependent on the individual. When, for example, he suggests that Christ can be born in the individual beyond the limiting features of the ego and the external world, we should understand this as a reference to the ontologically prior sphere of free energy in the light of which our whole mental apparatus appears as an agency of the dominant relations. These reserves in human nature can allow us to make a fresh start in the development of the species. My starting-point is simply that these psychic realities are material—a point of view perfectly consistent with historical materialism.

May we now turn to a more directly political aspect of your vision of cultural revolution. You have argued that parties must correspond to social classes and that this rules out a system of organizational pluralism. But even if we were to accept this position, it cannot be denied that there are at least two classes in any given proto-socialist society: the working class and the peasantry. Why, then, should there not be at least two political parties?

I can see that in Poland, for instance, where differences between the working class and peasantry have not narrowed as much as in the GDR, there may be a need for separate political representation of the peasantry. But, more generally, I envisage the Communist League of the future as a body that will be able to formulate a general perspective which goes beyond and reconciles different material interests.

Yes. But is this party or league to have a monopoly? From a psychological point of view, it is extremely unlikely that everyone will ever be in agreement; and although the Communist League will try to develop a synchronized programme, other people will want to do things in a different way. Will the people have no constitutional right to remove the Communist League and place another party in government?

My views on this are bound up with the questions we were discussing earlier. All these things—pluralism, the party system, the constitution, elections and so on—are posed in terms of the prevailing logic and dynamic of our civilization. It always seems to be forgotten that this type of political order and expression of interests has been a feature of societies in which commodity production, and most often capitalist commodity production, has been the norm; and that it therefore presupposes an underlying conflict of economic interests. My own position is that we must get away from this whole competitive struggle for economic interests. Once our material consumption is stabilized at a rational level, we will no longer think that bourgeois society is the best of all possible worlds.

But surely we are talking about a socialist *political pluralism, not bourgeois pluralism.*

As far as its basic logic is concerned, socialist pluralism is but an offshoot of bourgeois pluralism. According to Marx, communism is the overcoming of capitalist private property, and so it logically requires the prior existence of capitalist relations. This conception is, in my view, the source of socialist pluralism. And this is why, after the downfall of Stalinism, the idea appeared that we ought at last to consider the value of bourgeois democracy. I don't deny the usefulness of such an exercise, but it is rooted in the hitherto existing process of social development and cannot lay claim to some supra-historical validity. Previous societies have managed without all these political forms, and I believe that once man is living in harmony...

You now seem to be talking about a higher stage of communism.

No. I'm not referring to that theory of the stages of communism. I simply mean that we must get away from the logic of economic competition and reach a society where physical reproduction functions in the manner of a biological organism, where a basic level of real human needs is secured once and for all, and where politics and ideology can concern themselves with the development of the individual.

I don't wish to suggest, of course, that if there are two workers' parties, one of them will have to be destroyed. But I cannot imagine that *party pluralism* will be the answer to everything, because it is itself one of the mechanisms through which the present destructive dynamic is reproduced.

I remember that in our previous discussion you had a very positive assessment of the Eurocommunist phenomenon. What is your view today, now that you have been living in the West for two years or so?

The first thing that struck me was how close the Social Democrats and Eurocommunists are in matters of practical politics, for all their differences in ideology and tradition. The future of both currents, as of all socialist forces, will depend on how they face up to the crisis of the capitalist *industrial* system. The old pattern of contradictions and struggle always seems to lead back into the system, serving to reproduce it in its essential aspects. What we now need is an answer that goes beyond the traditional differences of approach between Social Democrats, Socialists and Communists. The old model has had its day.

You have now had quite an active experience of political life in West Germany, as well as knowing the social and political structure in the Eastern bloc. It is clear that the Western capitalist system remains a tremendous obstacle to the development towards communism, and also that the semi-repressive state structures in Eastern Europe are a barrier of a different kind. But how would you estimate the relative possibility of a breakthrough in Eastern and Western Europe?

What we have is a situation, expressed particularly clearly in the military field, where the two blocs not only stand in opposition to each other but actually stifle each other's possibilities of development. Neither of the two systems, as they are today, represents a viable option.

It would be illusory to expect some revolutionary initiative from the Eastern bloc: developments in Poland have revealed the crisis in the Soviet system and shown that it is generally on the wane. But I can see possibilities for reducing the power of those forces in the West that persist in the old patterns of cold war, anti-socialism and so on. The peace movement and ecology movement could help to break up these ossified structures, especially if the Social Democratic and Socialist forces were prepared to challenge their countries' commitment to the Western Alliance and other products of the Cold War mentality. This does not mean that they should align themselves with the Soviet camp, but that they should establish a status of non-alignment and neutrality, summoning Europe to help in solving the East-West, North-South and ecology crises. It may be that Europe, where industrial capitalism first developed, has more to contribute in this regard than the Soviet Union or Japan and the United States.

I am convinced that more and more people are questioning many old layers of our culture and pursuing the goal of radical change, because they are anxious to preserve certain things that are valuable to them. It is a process involving not just the peace movement or the search for European political neutrality but also questions of human relationships, of the environment, of Christianity, of the positive values residing in the working-class movement and so on. What we need is a sense of direction, a goal towards which to direct our efforts, however diverse these may be. My experience in West Germany has given me grounds for optimism, and I can see possibilities of combining a mass movement with pressure on certain individuals in the establishment. After all, we can't solve everything through a strategy of simple confrontation, and we have to differentiate between various kinds of people.

It seems clear that there is a significant interdependence of the situations in Western and Eastern Europe. The Russell Foundation grasped this with its reference to 'Europe from Poland to Portugal' (an entity which makes sense in historical and cultural terms alone), excluding the Soviet Union but not, of course, seeking to disregard its interests. Within this context we must consider direct, constructive plans of action and try to neutralize the main points of resistance and repressive obstruction on either side. It would be unproductive to over-emphasize the differences between East and West, since Western Europe cannot go it alone and, whatever the surface distinctions, the underlying crisis of the industrialist system grips the First, the Second and the Third World..

May we now turn to the question of Poland, which is of major importance in the present European situation. How do you see what has happened there in the last few months?

The problems had been swept under the carpet for so long in Poland that a primeval expression of immediate interests was almost inevitable. The Prague Spring, by contrast, involved a mediated process in which the various social forces found a programmatic reflection. Where political demands have arisen in Poland, these have also been of a trade-union type, directly expressing social interests. In Czechoslovakia the intellectuals, both inside and outside the Party, tended to run ahead of things, so that a global crisis did not overwhelm society in January 1968. But in Poland there really was a revolutionary crisis, in the sense that things could not go on as before, either at the top or at the bottom. Virtually all layers of society were drawn into the maelstrom.

The most difficult problem is to give a precise definition of Solidarnosc. The trade-union character of the working-class resistance helps to explain why it has no real political perspective of its own but just tries to exercise a veto and demands that the economic system should function properly. This means that political problems have been left to various fractions of the intelligentsia: above all those around KOR and those around the Catholic Church. In point of fact, the Church acts as an ideological force of at least equal weight to the Communist Party. The ad hoc political solutions that have been reached are the result of a confrontation between Party and state on the one hand, and the Church, the pro-Solidarity intellectuals and the working masses on the other. It was the workers' refusal to cooperate and their threats of strike action that forced the Party leadership to give way.

It is necessary to refer to the international situation, however, to explain why no hegemony has emerged—not even of the Church—and why no lasting national solution can be achieved.

Would you not agree that the working class has been the overwhelming force in the last few months? Of the events in Poland in 1970 you have written that the workers were atomized and incapable of acting as a class for itself. But things have changed since then; and as the old trade unions were incapable of representing the workers' interests, the working class has succeeded in forming its own union, with an independence which the government was forced to recognize in a written agreement. However great the weaknesses of Solidarity, the working class has clearly asserted its role as an independent class, with independent organizational forms. What you said in The Alternative *about the subordinate role played by the working class in capitalist as well as socialist or proto-socialist countries seems to be contradicted by what has happened in Poland.*

I don't see it in that way. True, the working class in Poland has found the strength to take the initiative. However, one cannot equate the working class in Poland with that in Western countries. It is important to see it within the relations of power in Poland itself, and not to draw conclusions that go beyond this limit.

When I wrote the chapter of my book about the inapplicability of the concept of the working class to proto-socialist society, I had already reflected on the role of the working class in the development of capitalism, including the German November Revolution of 1918 and the Kapp Putsch of 1920. In the November Revolution the working class acted as a kind of battering-ram but could not control the course of events or their outcome. In the same way I have never believed that the initiative of the Polish workers can produce a political solution to the problems of the moment. The working class is inserted in a parallelogram of forces in which its initiative is but one among many magnitudes.

A force no greater than others?

I regard both the Soviet Union and the West as more powerful forces in Poland.

But within Poland itself, surely the working class has proved to be the most important social force.

This is too mechanical a way of looking at the situation. Generally when one talks about classes, one is talking about combinations of quite specific interests. One pole of interests in Poland, which took the initiative in forcing a break in the political system, was the combination that found expression in the twenty-one demands of Solidarity. But there are also other interests present in the minds of those people who put forward Solidarity's programme. The Church is one case in point. But far more important, in my view, is what I call Western-style consumerism, which provides the horizon of 'the good life', of the use-values that should be generated in the overall reproduction process. Then the existence of the Soviet Union naturally plays an essential role, not only for the Communist Party but also for the actions of Lech Walesa. We need to trace all these intersecting combinations of interests as they are present in the minds of the individuals. But it does not seem to me that the whole process, in its international context, will produce results favouring what have traditionally been understood as working-class interests.

So what do you see as the most likely outcome of the crisis in Poland?

I'm afraid I can't see any hope of overcoming the economic crisis, given that the country is caught between the pressure of Western creditors and the Soviet veto on any political movement. Any solution would require that the national leadership—the Party, the government and the rest—gained genuine authority. But the sense of suspicion permeating the masses derives not only from official corruption but also from the regime's determination to keep Poland within the Soviet orbit—which is to the Poles a manifestation of the Soviet Union's domination of Poland and the whole of Eastern Europe. As long as this situation continues, the Poles will not be prepared to work for the government. The only possibility, and the natural tendency of national politics, is for Poland to leave the Warsaw Pact and become a kind of Yugoslavia, militarily independent.

There is very little evidence that the Polish masses are primarily concerned with the Soviet Union. Indeed, one might say the reverse, that they often show too little awareness of the possibility of some kind of Soviet intervention. Besides, why should Poland be tending in the direction of Yugoslavia? Why not Hungary, where the regime is more stable and there is less social unrest than in Yugoslavia?

For one thing the feeling of attachment to the nation is qualitatively stronger in Poland than in Hungary. For another, what national feeling there was in Hungary was crushed in the egg in 1956, and the urge to national self-assertion both expressed itself and played itself out in the fight against the Soviet Union. The Hungarians seem to have absorbed it into their system, not with any great pleasure, but they acknowledge the status quo and Kadar has only to point out the limits of the feasible for the people to accept it.

The stability of the Hungarian regime is ultimately rooted in economic well-being. Why should that be so impossible in Poland?

In 1956 the Hungarians quickly went back to work, because there was nothing else to do. In Poland there is no such clear situation, and without this clarity I can't see them finding a way out. The Russians can't intervene, unless they are prepared to destroy everything, and the Polish government can't be Polish and anti-Soviet enough to unite the people and get them back to work.

The Poles seem to be demanding two things. One is a reasonably efficient economic system that will provide them with the basic necessities and a decent supply of consumer durables. The other is a greater degree of political freedom, which will in turn permit the creation of a more efficient economic system. Not even Solidarity demands that Poland should leave the Warsaw Pact. Maybe the solution lies in a compromise between the Party on the one hand and Solidarity and the Church on the other. The prospects are not very bright that a sufficiently deep compromise will be reached to prevent great damage to the country. But that would seem to be the only rational course.

Let me just make it clear that I was not arguing for the Poles to leave the Warsaw Pact, just as I would not say that the juridical form of withdrawal from NATO is the most important question in the West. My only point is that I do not see the basis for a compromise. The Polish workers, in the broadest sense of the term, do not have the psychological make-up to say: 'Now let's get down to work', given the international situation, the extent of corruption and so forth.

Part Three

6
After the Elections

Let us begin by discussing the situation in Germany after the elections. The Greens are in Parliament but electorally the SPD is still much stronger. What is your assessment of the election result?

It was a conservative victory, but not a victory for the right from the point of view of the psychological motivation of the electorate. Realizing that the Social Democracy was finished, that it offered no solution to the deep social crisis, the average voter probably thought that Adenauer's offspring might be able to maintain his standard of living, help him keep up his mortgage payments and so on. This is actually Kohl's mandate from the electorate. Except for those with a totally alternative perspective, the CDU was the logical choice after the debacle of the Social Democrats.

We are dealing, I believe, with a conservative majority of 75 per cent, including half of those who voted SPD. Of course the SPD has the same aim: it's just that its promises are no longer credible. The CDU argument that 'we have the better relationship with Capital' was accepted by the electorate, not from any desire to add to the power of the capitalists, but because its experience of the 'German model' has taught it that the bigger the cake, the more there is for everyone. Given the present relationship of political forces, many have been persuaded that more profits are needed for investment, even though there has so far been no sign that increased profits lead to more jobs. In general it was argued very clearly, indeed with a certain realism, that labour is too expensive, that the strength of the trade unions affects export capacity, that there is a genuine conflict between the desire for higher wages and the need to export.

I don't believe that the election revealed any genuinely extremist tendencies in the population. Of course there are those who consider Strauss too tame, perhaps as many as twenty per cent in Bavaria, but that potential has always been there. There was no movement towards the fascist right. The conservative swing and even the attitude to immigrant workers are essentially a defensive reaction rather than an actively aggressive development. Fortunately external aggression is not a possible solution in the present international context, and the younger generation under forty has swung towards a completely different, less authoritarian form of social character. To this extent, I'm not really worried about any right-wing mobilization, although the government will try to restrict the scope of our activity and Interior Minister Zimmerman will take advantage of the violence in Krefeld to crack down on all demonstrations, even peaceful ones.

If three-quarters of the German population are conservative in their mentality and value system, what kind of perspective is there for the Left in Germany? After all, wasn't the election a defeat for the peace movement and the Greens? There may have been no real choice between the SPD and the CDU, but isn't this political continuity or stability a real danger for the eco-pacifist movement?

The election was certainly a defeat for the illusions of the peace movement. Now that the election is over, we have to begin to deal with the realities. There were many who voted CDU or FDP to prevent a red-green coalition. But they did so not because they wanted the missiles, but because economically the red-green coalition had nothing to offer. Even in the most favourable circumstances the Greens could only have subordinated themselves to the piecemeal reformist projects of the SPD, thus continuing the downward course of the Schmidt-Lambsdorff period. The Greens would have taken on the role of the FDP, merely pulling the SPD from the opposite side.

The popular support for German capitalism, or rather for the continuity of the economic order, runs very deep indeed. The alternative is a black hole. No one wants the Federal Republic to sink to the level of Britain, and no one believed that the SPD and the Greens could do anything but oversee a further decline. But if the economic question was in the foreground, this was because a solution to the arms race and the ecological crisis does not yet appear realistic.

As far as the question of peace is concerned, I think we were a little too optimistic about the people's perception of the war danger. There is a gradual realization that the arms madness has gone far enough and that the danger may increase with the new missiles, but there is also a conviction that the bomb has kept the peace since 1945, that we can't make unilateral concessions, and that in any case there's no proof that the alternative would be any better. Although the polls showed 61 per cent against the missiles, we forgot that just a year before the election 75 per cent of the population had still wanted to be defended by the Americans.

Is there a real contradiction between those figures?

Of course.

For us, yes, but for them?

Well, people don't realize that the only defence which the first atomic superpower can give is nuclear defence. So if they need to be defended, and want to be, then they'll get the missiles the Americans want to station here. The fundamental consensus concerning defence of the free West, and especially West Germany, against the totalitarian East is dented but not broken. The Russell Appeal, or the conflict with the DKP (West German Communist Party) within the peace movement, is not perceived by the majority of the people. Strauss can therefore brand us as friends of the Soviets, although this is becoming more difficult. Our action on Alexanderplatz, for example, when Petra Kelly and Bastian demonstrated against missiles East and West, was an event of considerable importance. We also attended the Prague conference and met with Charter 77. So people are beginning to realize that we oppose military policy in the East as well as the West, that the course we pursue is our own.

You have argued in the peace movement against crude anti-Sovietism, against the view that the USA and the USSR have an equal responsibility for the arms race.

Yes. I have always rejected the idea of equal responsibility or the argument that the Russians are coming. But much more important than the differences between the systems is the fact that, with respect to the arms race, they constitute a single system, within which the Soviet Union is the dependent variable.

You don't consider the social systems in the Soviet Union and the West to be the same?

No, we don't need to discuss that. We call for disarmament East and West—which gives the appearance that we equate the two systems. Let's disarm East and West. Let's begin here. That, quite simply, is our slogan.

Is that the generally accepted slogan of the Greens, or only of one section?

That is the general position, although some of us place greater emphasis on unilateralism, on the struggle against American missiles here. The anti-imperialist and the pro-Soviet arguments converge to some extent, but the motives are different. There are some people in the Greens who consider any criticism of Soviet military policy to be a concession to the Americans. This is wrong in practice, because such a policy on our part would only strengthen Reagan's position. It is also theoretically false: if it's a single system, then it doesn't matter at which point you enter the vicious circle; it will work both ways anyway. We can liberate Europe only by applying the pressure in both directions. Of course the popular impression is that to push Reagan back is to create a vacuum for the Russians. This anti-communism has a cultural component which is very difficult to overcome if we deal with it in the traditional manner. For it involves opposition not simply to the Soviet type of socialism but to the culturally alienating form developed by the Soviets and, by means of the state planned economy, imposed on Eastern Europe. On its own, Eastern Europe would probably have developed a different cultural form, and it reacts to this transplant in much the same way that the body does to a transplanted organ. Furthermore, the Russian Revolution was the first anti-colonial revolution, the first counteroffensive against European expansionism for centuries. In other words, it was the response of the non-capitalist world to our civilization as a whole, and in particular to the European form of individualism. It is this individualism which feels itself threatened.

I believe that this feeling stems mainly from the fact that it was an anti-capitalist revolution. Then there are specific reasons in Germany for this anti-communism—for instance, the Second World War and the colonial past.

I think you overestimate the anti-socialist factor. Consider the German Social Democracy at the end of the last century, a period of unimpeded growth despite the shock of the Commune. The fear of socialism didn't grip the German working class then: it became a dominant factor only after the Second World War, when the attitude of the West European working class came to resemble the hostility of the Roman lower classes towards the barbarian. This cultural history has a greater significance than we often appreciate. The Soviet model confronts the form of individuality of the entire European civilization, including the European working class. The famous freeborn Englishman, regardless of class, could not accept this model.

The peace movement is in a much more favourable situation now, in spite of the election results. The younger generation especially, but in fact West Germany as a whole, has had its attention focused so much on the Third World in recent decades that the North–South dimension has moved much more into the foreground relative to the East–West conflict. The problem is perceived more and more from the standpoint that the European social order itself is at fault, and that the next generation will have more reason to fear missiles from the South than from the East.

There are a number of possibilities here. A third world war could begin in the Third World if conflict between the United States and the Soviet Union breaks out in that region. The NATO countries could also go to war against a Third World country, for instance Iran, and this would be more in keeping with the history of the past two centuries. Of course it is also possible that some Third World country could acquire nuclear weapons and use them against the developed capitalist countries. But why do you emphasize this third possibility when, historically, the first two are much more likely?

I don't see it quite that way. Of course in the short term you are right, but in a longer historical perspective the third possibility is very great. If we look at the final centuries of the Roman Empire, we see that it was its policy towards outlying regions that led to its downfall. And the lower classes, who strongly supported this policy, were the hardest hit by it.

Consider the ecology movement here in Germany. If it receives so much sympathy from people whom you might want to call narrow-minded and middle-class, this is because the forest they see from their front window is disappearing, because the house in which they have invested thirty years' income will lose its value when the motorway comes through, and because now the missiles are about to arrive. You can't go to those people with the simple argument that we ought not to attack the Russians again. You can say it, and maybe they'll give it a moment's thought, but what really strikes home is the risk to themselves in the whole affair. When I came here in 1979, the Iranian revolution was already underway and a majority of people supported the intervention of some kind of Rapid Deployment Force to prevent oil prices rising still further. The social consensus, then, although not always so blatantly interventionist, is primarily concerned to maintain the status quo in the metropolitan centre. Our main emphasis must be placed on the disaster we're preparing for ourselves if we go on like this, with the weapons, the industrial system and the present standard of living.

Objectively there's some truth in what you say. According to official US security sources thirty countries in the Third World will have nuclear weapons by the end of the century. But isn't there a form of racism inherent in your argument that the main danger is from the blacks, the yellows? Who needs Gaddafy when we've got Reagan? I see the logic of your argument that this response from the Third World would be a direct result of the militarism of our own society. But with your conclusions on the main danger I don't agree.

And yet the danger is there. I believe that an important contribution which the peace movement can make is to shift the emphasis away from the obsessive East–West problem towards our whole relationship with the South. When you consider the relatively small disturbance in German society which was required to bring Hitler to power, and when you think of the enormous disruption we inflict on the peoples of the southern hemisphere with our economic and weapons systems, it will hardly be surprising if we soon end up with a multipolar system of terror. Egon Bahr tells us that the bipolar system of mutual terror is now under control. We don't believe that, and in fact the whole metropolitan-imperialist model is heading towards multipolarity, with all its potentially disastrous consequences. Since the majority of people do not respond to appeals for altruism or solidarity, the argument has to be broadened from the question of peace to the environment and our relations with the Third World. The Pershings are indeed an image of our total situation, for here we are setting up things whose essential characteristic is that they could eventually destroy us.

You're saying, in other words, that the Romans must transform their own institutions and establish a better relation with the Goths and the Vandals.

That's exactly what I am saying. In a recent discussion with Galtung, I argued that there was an aggressive Indo–Germanic disposition inherent in our European civilization which was already displayed by the Hittites in Asia Minor, the Greeks at Troy, and the Germanic tribes in their struggle against Rome. Galtung refers to this character-type as *homo occidentalis*, further defining the Nazi *homo conquistador* as an extreme variant of this. The necessity of a profound transformation in European civilization implies that this *homo occidentalis* or *homo conquistador* must be spiritually exorcised.

I have only mentioned this because I believe that the Western way of life has a profoundly expansive character, that capitalism has merely been a historical instrument whereby this disposition is advanced. No other civilization has created an economic order of such efficiency and aggressiveness that the system itself is a threat to the common interests of humanity.

In your view, then, a discussion of the North–South axis, of the danger from the South rooted in the North's industrialism, is useful to the peace movement as a way of combating the typical anti-Soviet conservatism and shifting the emphasis away from the East–West conflict.

I want to relativize the alleged danger from the East, so that we can cast more light on the East–West model of Freedom versus Totalitarianism which we've been offered up to now. People forget that it was Hitler who brought the Russians to the Elbe. They don't understand that the Russian Revolution was a response to the challenge from Europe, that there is a continuity from Peter the Great to Lenin, that the Russian Revolution was an anti-colonial revolution.

The quest for a new form of argumentation that takes us away from anti-Soviet Atlanticism is of great strategic importance for the peace movement. But there is also another problem, not so much for the peace movement as for the Greens: namely, the economic crisis whose principal result is unemployment. Those millions of unemployed want to work; they want growth, they want more and not less industry. But as you are against industry, against growth and development, there is a suspicion in the popular consciousness not only that you are friends of the Soviet Union but also that you have no jobs to offer. How would you answer that point?

It is certainly a major problem. At the crucial conference of the Greens last autumn I attacked the section of the draft programme on unemployment because it was completely based on the traditional left social-democratic model. Then I wrote something, very rapidly, in which I said that unemployment releases energies from the old bonds, that it gives us the opportunity to provide the unemployed with a new perspective. Of course the polemic developed in such a way that I was soon said to be arguing that five million unemployed are five million opportunities to climb out of the industrial system. The CDU then used this quotation against us in its election propaganda. But at the second conference in Sindelfingen we agreed on a programme which mainly called for a 35-hour week, together with new types of investment, protection of the environment and so on.

The situation now is that we have an eco-reformist, and thus left social-democratic programme. In the Preamble we still maintain that we have too much and not too little industry, but we specify where we think the excesses are and what other things might be more desirable. After this rather broad and ecological preamble, there is the immediate programme of twenty-one pages, of which nineteen and a half deal with piecemeal repairs to the system. Only one and a half pages deal with alternative projects such as eco-communities, communal work and so on—in other words, answers that lie beyond the factory.

An important factor here was that among the Greens, who are mostly very young people, the Marxist tradition has the greatest expertise on questions of political economy. As a result we now have an economic programme which, in its concrete measures, even Eppler couldn't improve on. In the election campaign we found ourselves fighting over who had stolen what from whom.

Now that the elections are over, I would say that our documented interest in the problem of unemployment played a significant role in attracting votes from people oriented towards the SPD. No other party called for a 35-hour week—a demand which the DGB trade-union federation has now adopted. Ninety-four per cent of the population chose between the SPD and the CDU on the basis of the economic considerations we have already discussed. The people who voted Green, however, rejected this schema that the economy was the main question at stake. They saw that the Greens were somewhat chaotic, but they also saw that we were against the arms race and the destruction of the environment. Hans-Jochen Vogel, leader of the SPD, maintained that the Greens ask all the right questions, while the SPD has all the right answers. Yet our economic programme is not so bad. The Greens remain both fundamentalist and reformist, and our internal dispute is not about whether we should support the economic measures in the immediate programme, but about what our priorities should be. Our main concerns cannot be the old questions of capitalist politics: whether pensions are adequate, whether mothers should draw a child allowance and so on. With our small numbers we can't fight on the same front as the DGB does with its millions of members. We must use our strength for something else: to be the instrument of a new orientation beyond the conflicts of supply-and-

172

demand politics.

But you must offer something. Although the economy may not always be the main priority, it is nonetheless an important question for the majority of people in Germany and England. The fact that the Greens are against economic growth is both a fundamental philosophical problem and a concrete electoral one.

It wasn't such a big problem in this election because political-economic cooperation between reds and greens was anyway not a serious possibility. Maybe in the future, if the Greens develop into a politically relevant force, the economic question will become decisive and I hope we will have made it clear that the forests can't be saved by marginally reducing the emission of industrial chemicals into the air. The Vogelsberg near Frankfurt is being destroyed by Frankfurt's industry. It is becoming more and more apparent that our industrial system is incompatible with the preservation of our natural environment. Things are now reaching the point where you can begin to say to people: you must choose between the industrial system and the German forest. You can't have both. We will be forced, in the future, to undertake a complete transformation of our civilization, right down to its material foundations. That is what I am saying.

We will come to that later. I would like now just to discuss the political problems of the post-election period. Since you are opposed not only to the pollution of the environment but also to growth and industry itself, you would seem to place yourselves in opposition to work as such, and to people earning an income. We have spoken of the depth of anti-Sovietism and the way it was historically conditioned and established in German society, and you say that the form of European individualism has a lot to do with this. But doesn't your attitude to industrialism also come into conflict with this 'European' individualism, and even with a basic, universal human desire for material goods?

When you call the dominant life-style into question, you come up against a whole series of things which are bound together in this structure of individuality. For instance, if you want to introduce a speed-limit on the autobahn, you run up against the slogan 'free road for a free citizen' (*freie Fahrt für freie Bürger*). To some extent 1968 marked the beginning of a change in attitudes, so that progress and freedom and happiness are no longer so simply identified with further growth. The consensus now is more of a negative one: Kohl's task is to hold off the collapse of the system because we don't know what kind of a black hole we'll fall into if it does collapse. In essence, however, the attitude is still that what you want, and what you can pay for, you should get. The ideological battle is now taking place around the Greens' call for renunciation, for self-limitation, and I don't think that we are entirely without success. In fact, the Greens are the expression of the cultural shift that has occurred since 1968, and the debates inside the Greens are about how we should politically deal with this. In other words, should we be provocative and say we have to dismantle the industrial system? Or should we lure the electorate, step by step, with small corrections to the system?

The Greens can grow now because there is no danger that we will put our plans into effect. The central question is how we transform the consensus. Many of our own members are annoyed when I say that their conception of gradually inching forward is a social-democratic course, and that it is both necessary and possible to reach the point of decisive change more quickly. I would like to make clear what we seek to achieve. On the missiles question, for example, we should openly say not only that nuclear disarmament in Europe will change our relation with the Soviet Union, but also that we will have to have a completely different relation with the Third World from that which the Americans have. We must also explain that it is impossible to get rid of capitalism and emerge from the crisis while holding on to the welfare state that has been built up from the time of Bismarck. Doing away with the Welfare State is not, of course, the *first* task. Unemployment can only be an opportunity if you don't have to go begging the next day, if you can devote time over the next six months to thinking about fundamental questions. Am I a proper human being only when I stand on the assembly line? Do I have to go back to that? Is my main concern wage-labour and income? Or is it the maintenance of life, something essentially natural? It would have a completely different logic if we were to present ourselves as a movement campaigning against cuts in child allowances, for higher pensions, and so on; in other words, to deal only with immediate social questions in the manner of a trade union. That is without any historical perspective. The key question is therefore one of priorities.

It may be possible to achieve agreement on priorities. But you also have the problem of political mediation, of communication. You are critical of professionalism in politics, of the professional politicians who in the name of realism concern themselves with day-to-day political decisions. But now that the Greens are in Parliament, how can you stand aside from that kind of politics?

If we had won a majority with the SPD, we would be completely tied up with such matters. As things stand, however, nothing depends on us in this Parliament: the CDU and FDP will always have a majority. In local politics (town councils, community councils etc.), where the prejudices we face are those of ordinary people rather than of the political apparatuses, we have to deal with issues in a much more concrete way. But in the Bundestag the link with everyday reality is very weak. There are stacks of paper piled on every desk, and if we were to try to work through all of them, we would lose our way quite soon. All the problems are so structured in advance by the power relations that there is no possibility of changing the direction of draft legislation. The most we could do is try to uncover the deceptions in the small print and to find out what the legislation really means. For instance, Zimmerman is supposed to have drafted a law restricting the emission from power-stations, but, according to my reading of it, he has allowed it to be actually increased. In fact, one of the reasons why I am pleased with the election results is that we now have time to clarify and put forward our distinctive identity, instead of tying ourselves down in surface politics and engaging in acrimonious exchanges with the SPD. (Vogel would, for instance, have undoubtedly put his name to the Williamsburg Declaration.) It is important that the population should come to understand that we have our own particular standpoint, that we are not just sometimes with the SPD and sometimes with the CDU. Now we can choose whether we want to stay with the radical-liberal positions of people like Otto Schiele or Jorschke Fischer or whether we can develop a more fundamental op-

positional politics in the sense of Gramsci, in other words at the level
of cultural and ideological hegemony and not of emissions from
power stations.

You're not opposed to the presence of the Greens in the Bundestag?

No. I was only opposed to my own presence there. The parliamentary fraction now has incredible political weight in relation to the
Greens as a whole, whereas the Green Party itself is organizationally
much more spread out at the base. It's important that the fraction
doesn't lose the link with the movement, that the discussion is built
up from the base in such a way as to prevent the fraction from
becoming too absorbed in Realpolitik. And I think the situation is
favourable for us in this respect. I have the very strong impression
that the cultural trend in 1968 is actually accelerating: those who
voted Green have, in their thinking, come more than fifty per cent of
the way in our direction; while those who have now come only ten
per cent towards us will in four years have come thirty per cent. The
election results give absolutely no indication of this psychological
shift. Even the CDU and the SPD go out of their way to present
themselves as ecologists; the phraseology of peace is on everyone's
lips. They even try to convince young people that Reagan's only concern is to strengthen the peace. And Kohl is not entirely unsuccessful
in this—after all, Reagan doesn't look like someone who could impose martial law.

As I said at the SPD Congress in Munich last April, it will take
some time for the CDU to reveal through its practice that everything
wasn't just the fault of the SPD, that the German Model itself is
finished. The CDU may survive beyond 1987 but not beyond 1991.
That's my prognosis. Already, whenever I speak to a German au-
dience and say that another thirty-five years of the old kind of industrialization will finish us all, it is surprising how readily people
agree. It will soon be clear to everyone that further investment is not
going to alter the basic unemployment situation. They can build
more motorways or extend the Rhine–Danube Canal—and that may
bring in some profits, even help to maintain our market abroad and
ensure that there's enough money for unemployment insurance. But
according to all the data I have seen, it will not conjure away the four

million unemployed. The only chance would be the very rapid introduction of a 35-hour week, not offset by further rationalization. A gradual transition to the 35-hour week would not bring unemployment down because it could be achieved through rationalization. It is in fact optimistic to think that there will be only four million unemployed in 1990.

The crucial point, however, is that unemployment no longer causes the same hopelessness that it did twenty years ago. The existence of the Green alternative is an important factor in this. Unemployment is not just a crisis of need, then or now, but a crisis of identity for the individual. The immediate impression is that, out of work, you are a nobody. But according to social workers involved in this field, many young people begin to feel after a few months, or maybe half a year, that perhaps work isn't the most important thing after all, that it is necessary to rediscover themselves, make a new circle of friends, and so on. Among at least half of the young generation today the search for identity through a career is definitely on the decline.

You have spoken about 1968, which was above all a period of extraparliamentary action. But now the Greens look for seats in Parliament. Do you think that the kind of social transformation or revolution you have been describing will come through Parliament? Or is Parliament only a tribune, so that the revolution will require other instruments, other institutions? What is the role of Parliament in Green strategy?

It is difficult to compare the role of Parliament in England and Germany. Perhaps in England it is difficult to imagine institutional change bypassing Parliament, but in Germany it is quite easy to imagine that it will be not only extra-parliamentary but antiparliamentary. It is another question whether that's a good thing. The Social Democrats often accuse the Greens of being hostile to the ‚ystem in the way that the Nazis were. I would say that this is not true of the Greens, although there are in the ecological and peace movement forces that are not so much anti-parliamentary as antiinstitutional. There is a danger in this, because it confuses the sphere of the state with the sphere of law.

I am in favour of a peaceful transition. I don't mean peaceful in opposition to the old revolutionary theory because that just doesn't work anyway—there is no danger of mass insurrection. By peaceful I mean without war, without external aggression, without conflict over scarce natural resources. A peaceful transition is one in which the fundamental elements of a legal order are not destroyed. I see no need to destroy the institutional structure, and I want to get away from the terminology of violence. I think of the process as one of dissolution, passive from the point of view of the subject of this dissolution. We don't go in and disband something: we allow it to disintegrate by withdrawing our energy from the system as such. I do not believe this is a non-materialist viewpoint, for, considered monistically, psychic energy, living labour or the spirit is material and perhaps more important than money or machinery.

As far as Parliament is concerned, this is linked to what I said earlier about the need to change the consensus in the metropolitan centres. In the final analysis the lower classes have always been part of the foreign policy consensus because they have a vital interest in the continuing functional capacity of the system as a whole. The election has demonstrated that once again. We can't go to people and ask them to act against their own fundamental interests, but we must focus on the contradiction between their immediate short-term interests and their long-term, fundamental interests. For instance, today you have to pay off the mortgage on your house, and for that you risk that your children won't live to be thirty, whether from bombs or from the poisoning of the environment. We are in such a situation now that the long-term interests directly affect even the children. So our policy must be, not directly to attack the expressions of this consensus, but to make people aware of the basic contradiction. Such a change in the consensus will involve a new institutionalization and legal legitimation, although we should not exaggerate the anti-institutional aspect. From this point of view, perhaps the only intelligent input that we had from the allied occupation after 1945 was the conception of a legal order which no longer needs to be guaranteed by authoritarianism. That I regard as progress, especially in Germany.

There was the Frankfurt Parliament of 1848.

Yes, but it wasn't able to achieve stability.

But it wasn't just General Eisenhower who achieved this.

That's not what I mean. It wasn't the troops who did this, it was rather a question of cultural contact, which was something positive. I'm not praising the economic motives, the Marshall Plan or the power-political interests. I simply mean that after 1945 the Anglo-Saxon tradition played a positive cultural role. The younger generation of today doesn't have the same conflict-orientation that was characteristic of the old and new left of 1968. They are more Anglo-Saxon, in the sense of having a greater tolerance for a diversity of opinions. There is greater acceptance of diversity of thought, of pluralism and the ability to unite around an agreed goal. This appears to me to be politically and culturally very important.

The problem, then, is not whether we overestimate Parliament or consign it to the dustbin. The problem is how we can change the ideological, cultural and psychological consensus, and it will be of some interest to see how this new task is articulated in Parliament. The usefulness of Parliament to us now is not that it enables us to work towards the famous 51 per cent, without which even Berlinguer wouldn't govern, but that it allows us to drive home our message, our challenge to popular consciousness. In this sense its primary function is still, if you wish, that of a tribune. But in the workers' movement it was always class against class, whereas now something is debated which is of interest to the entire society. We are the organ not of any particular interest but of the general interest. We are against the established interests, however, and most strongly against the interests of capital, the big corporations and the state. When the ecological viewpoint has been considered, there will certainly be practical compromises with the eco-industry or bio-industry, and we will probably still have the computer. This ecological peace movement is the answer of the younger generation to the Second World War, containing the most active emancipatory elements of this society. Of course we have to compete with such right-wing manifestations as the hostility to foreign workers, but we are already ahead in that battle. And I am certain that, precisely on this point, we will lose the possibility of winning hegemony if we proceed along the old left-wing lines. Anti-fascism is not enough. In fact it would only strengthen such forces by raising the fences behind which they could really organize.

Do you think that in the future the Greens will actually form a government? Or will they, when they come to power, get rid of Parliament and build new institutions? The Greens exist in a space between the spontaneist-anarchist movement, which is opposed to all institutions, and the Leninists who see Parliament as an instrument of class rule that has to be destroyed. You reject both positions, but in the final analysis you must have some policy on those institutions.

What was left, in institutional terms, at the end of the Roman Empire? The Christian Church simply took its place.

The main emphasis of a new institutionalization must be on the economic level. Anarchism, self-management and so on are absurd if you are dealing with corporations that serve a world market, have branches in seventeen countries and contain ten separate levels of management. Although self-management may have some value as a form of ideological resistance, it will have no effect in this kind of situation.

The old industrial system is at an end: the increase in material consumption and production, with the inbuilt waste, pollution and depletion of resources, has reached its *non plus ultra* and is enough to destroy us in a few generations. Here in Bremerhaven we unload cars from Japan and load cars for America. The amount of material consumed per capita is now ten times higher than it was in the time of Schiller, not because individuals consume so much more but because of the massive material infrastructure of the world market. We must now enter into a phase of contraction, which in the first instance has to be economic. If I may pick an arbitrary figure, let us take an area fifty by a hundred kilometres wide. It must be possible to organize reproduction at this level: food, homes, schools, clothing, medicine, perhaps as much as ninety per cent of what we need. For another nine per cent we could deal on a national or provincial level, and for the further one per cent we would be dependent on a world market.

So you are against the world market and for autarkic national development.

What I imagine is that this world-market material infrastructure could be replaced by a world-market informational structure. In other words communication would remain but material transport would disappear, although of course not all at once.

Do you want this for all countries of the world or only for more favourably situated countries like Germany that are large, have plenty of resources, and so on? What if I live in Singapore or Upper Volta?

What I am describing is only the general tendency. According to what I have read, for instance in the statistically informed work of Johan Galtung, self-reliance is a better prospect for Third World countries than it is for us... so long as we leave them alone and cease to exploit them.

But autarky and exploitation are not the only options. Indeed, I would say that Galtung's concept of self-reliance is not possible for any country, while non-exploitative trade, involving exchange on a mutually beneficial basis, is a perfectly conceivable possibility. What you are proposing for Germany is more or less autarky and a self-reliant economy.

I may have exaggerated in talking of a reduction from 100 to 1. Some countries may need external trade to the magnitude of, say, ten per cent. But, to carry this to its logical conclusion, it already makes economic sense to think of producing certain types of necessary goods at one particular point in the world, from which global distribution could then take place. What I want to underline is the principle of contraction and the dissolution of the world market as we know it. If we want to achieve equilibrium and stability, we may have to re-create the original structure of the world market, which was limited to a small quantity of surplus and luxury goods. The challenge to Germany is to attain simple reproduction, without having to import apple juice from Morocco and without all this EEC agricultural policy.

I have inserted these thoughts because it is only on this basis that I can answer your question about Parliament. If this 'economic' strategy is successful, it will bring a shift of power from the top towards the base. The utopian or ideal solution would be completely to reverse the relationship whereby local authorities are hopelessly dependent on the central authority so that the representative element or structure, bringing together accountable rank-and-file delegates, would be a question not of legal statute but of the real social relations. If the centre of gravity of production is at the base, then it doesn't matter what you call the representative institution. I have often said that we couldn't have a better flag than the rainbow banner of Thomas Münzer in the Peasant War.

The real point is that it is first of all through the 'roundabout' way of culture or subjectivity that we can arrive at a new institutionalization. We are helped in this of course by the fact that the present institutions demonstrate their inability to save the situation. They are constructed in such a way that if you don't want the missiles and the new motorways then you can only opt out. The scope of legitimation becomes even smaller. Just as in the Weimar Republic, the deterioration of the political system itself is an issue of debate. And in a certain respect, the Greens are playing a regenerative role at the level of legality or legitimation. It could be that we will be sucked in, that we will only provide an injection for the sick body. But it could also be that, in the rupture, we will provide a certain institutional continuity as far as the real content is concerned. That there already exists a deficit of legitimation is demonstrated by the discussions about the need for a parallel institution, a kind of citizens' parliament. Of course the average citizen is first of all looking for some ecological repairs to the German Model. But the system cannot deliver this: expansion, the welfare state, the whole thing is turning sour. Even if there is some quantitative growth, more people will fall into the welfare net, and achievements will diminish while the bureaucratic apparatus expands. Thus, in a manner completely different from the past, a problem of dual power will arise, some form of parallel institutionalization if not actually an alternative parliament. The idea of a citizens' parliament is a way of expressing the fact that although the old Parliament is no longer functional, we do not wish to think in terms of dissolving it. I have met with similar conceptions in America, the most interesting aspect of which was that the parallel institutions were to have completely different tasks from those of the older bodies. As the consensus in society shifts to one of social justice without growth, without sharpening of class struggle, it will be interesting to see the way in which this is expressed institutionally. The Greens, unlike the obsolete traditional parties, are an element in the process through which a new institutionalization, with a new *content*, is being prepared. What we have to ensure is that this supersedes the image of aggressive disruption that much of the population still associates with us.

Our problem here is that society is looking for an orderly transition. Everything must be radically transformed if we want everything to stay as it is, as someone said. This is the point to which everything is leading. There is still a tendency, for instance, to respond to the problem of unemployment by saying 'wages and bread for everyone'—in other words, 'reproduce the world market and so on'. Up to now we have considered redistribution within the system. What we really have to deal with is redistribution out of the system: redistribution on a totally different foundation, not capitalist and, I would even say, not European. Galtung's concept of self-reliance is not European because its aim is simple reproduction. The European conception is expanded reproduction or expansion in its most elementary sense.

How European are the Japanese?

According to Galtung's analysis they are super-European. The Japanese economy had natural conditions similar to ours, as well as the only feudal structure outside Europe.

You don't seem to want to admit that there are important class interests in capitalist society which would fight against such a transformation. On the other hand, the forces of an alternative, based on class interests, will have to organize themselves. What role do you see in your movement for traditional working-class organizations such as the trade unions?

Let us go back again to Rome. Writing from the standpoint of class relations in nineteenth-century Europe, Marx recognized that the Roman class struggle always revolved round the agrarian question and constituted the productive stimulus of the entire development. But at the end of the Roman period, as Marx or perhaps Engels observed, there was deadlock between two classes, neither of which represented the new society. Neither the free men of the Asiatic mode of production, nor the slaves of antiquity, nor the peasants under feudalism were the representatives of the new society that was to develop. Similarly, within feudal society both the bourgeois and the free labourer were formed through a process of disintegration of the old society, of the old formation. Yet it wasn't the bourgeois class which created or bore the new formation. It may have played the most active part, but I believe that the development of a new formation out of the old is the best way of describing what happened.

Now, the Marxist hypothesis is that this time it is the proletariat which is the bearer of the new society, although there is the problem that the proletariat will then cease to be a proletariat. I think it has become very doubtful that the proletariat within bourgeois society will be the bearer or the subject of the new society. At the end of this capitalist formation, the problem is not the abolition of the bourgeois class but the dissolution of the whole formation constituted by wage-labour and capital. However, the confrontation of wage-labour and capital is not the mechanism of this dissolution. Such confrontation does not exist. Without the support of the metropolitan working class colonialism would not have been possible, and it is the position and strength of the trade unions which have given stability to the whole system here. It is the industrial system itself which is about to undo us—not the bourgeois class but the system as a whole in which the working class plays the role of housewife. It would therefore be a most inappropriate strategy for survival to appeal to the interests of the working class. Expansion during the time of the Caesars was driven forward by the need to pacify the lower classes; and today it is hard to say whether the small entrepreneur or the worker has the greater interest in building something like the West Runway at Frankfurt airport. In Berlin construction workers demonstrated against the squatters because they wanted jobs modernizing the squatted houses. The working class here is the richest lower class in the world. And if I look at the problem from the point of view of the whole of humanity, not just from that of Europe, then I must say that the metropolitan working class is the worst exploiting class in history.

In this context, let us take the example of a city on the coast of Africa, a bridgehead of the metropolis. In order to drive their Mercedes, the ruling bureaucrats must dispossess the peasantry in the hinterland and create a working class in the city. Supermarkets are built and a system of monoculture brought in. But what happens when there is no more hinterland to exploit? What made poverty bearable in eighteenth or nineteenth-century Europe was the prospect of escaping it through exploitation of the periphery. But this is no longer a possibility, and continued industrialism in the Third World will mean poverty for whole generations and hunger for millions. The perspective of proletarianizing humanity is a horrific vision. I have accented this rather polemically and of course you will say that the capitalists also have something to do with this, not just the workers. But just as in the case of the missiles, where it's no longer enough to say 'it's the fault of the Americans' because the problem is the whole vicious circle in which both Russians and Americans revolve, so also in the case of capitalism the workers are part of the carousel of the capitalist formation. The problem for humanity is how to put an end to this industrial-capitalist formation as a whole. I no longer ask the workers to expropriate the capitalists because that won't work. The radicalism required for this task does not exist in the metropolis. They have more to lose than their chains, much more. And so, the message to the capitalists, but especially to the workers, the wage-earners in the widest sense, is that they must climb out of this vicious circle.

To speak in traditional terms, the time has come when the utopian communist and socialist visions are no longer utopian. We have reached the limit. Nature will not accept any more and it's striking back. The external proletariat, in Toynbee's sense, won't let itself be exploited anymore, and herein lies the danger. The internal proletariat still has the strength to demand more bread and leisure, but that too has its limits. As to the problems of subjectivity, psychiatry is becoming less and less a solution, and some kind of more communal practice will have to emerge. Marx and Lenin both maintained that human productivity will only be unchained when it is set free of wage labour. But Marx was still very much a man of the bourgeois period, of European civilization, in that he laid stress on objectivity or the making of things. This making of things has acquired an independence of its own, so that material expansion has become a cultural characteristic of Europeans. We must now begin to think of simple reproduction: we can no longer think of progress in terms of one kilo of steel or concrete today, two kilos tomorrow.

I have noticed in your writings that you are very critical of the trade unions. What role do you envisage for them in the campaign of the Greens?

The trade unions belong to the most conservative forces in society. Their whole structure, which creates the army for the conflict with capital, sets them in opposition to this transformation of society. The orientation towards the factory weakens the trade unions, as does the present crisis. Subjectively and institutionally historical development has weakened corporatism. I see the ecology and peace movement as a contrast to the trade-union structure.

You are saying that it is the inner structure of the unions, not the leadership, which makes them necessarily conservative?

Exactly. They are objectively bound to the system as one component of the power complex. Viewed from the outside, the opposition between the trade unions and the employers' organizations is relative, the opposition of the whole set-up to the interests of humanity is absolute. In a crisis of the economic system, when the task is to overcome this formation in its totality, we cannot rely upon an organization in which the second industrial class is organized as a class. Of course political activity by the Greens and the eco-peace movement among trade unionists is a different question. We already do this and we must take advantage of every opportunity. For instance, I was invited to the Ruhr Festival, a yearly event organized by the trade unions, to debate with Ernest Mandel. I certainly don't ignore those people, but I go there in order to put a question-mark over trade-union structures and to draw people towards my position. The older the industry which the union represents, the more conservative it is. The most conservative here are the miners.

Do the actual organizations of the working class have no role to play in the campaign to make the Green programme a reality?

No. My attitude is that we should look positively on the disintegration of those organizations. It is not our task to destroy them or anything like that, but nor is it our job to help to restabilize them. I don't want human energy wasted on a dying problem. I want to break through this whole discourse. The political conceptions of the labour movement must disappear, and the human energies that have sought emancipation by this route must be redirected along another path.

In The Alternative *you opposed pluralism or a multi-party system under socialism, and you defended this position in an earlier interview with us. Your concern now is with the transformation of capitalism rather than of actually existing socialism. How do you see the problem of pluralism in a Green society?*

The whole discussion of pluralism reflects the differentiation that exists and is given expression in bourgeois society. Trade unions and employers' organizations exist, and although I believe that wage labour and capital should disappear, it is not our task as Greens to eliminate this representation of different interests. The point is, however, that the recognition of pluralism takes place at a level which merely mirrors this society's past.

We must be clear that democracy is an achievement of bourgeois society which, despite superstructural phenomena of confrontation, is in essence the form in which the competition between different claims in the distribution process is worked through. When the cake is only so big, and the relation of forces is more or less stable, this struggle of interests inevitably leads to colonialism. This is the best way to make the cake bigger or to keep it from growing smaller. So the question of pluralism or democracy in this sense should not be confused with the problem of how a community-oriented society would give expression to its own real contradictions. I imagine that such a society will be based on smaller units, that it will be much easier to establish consensus by discussion, that there will be a higher level of agreement over fundamental interests, and that competition between different interests will not take place at the fundamental level of social organization. In other words, the area requiring an equilibrium of different interests will be much smaller. I find here in West Germany—as opposed to the GDR, or Africa for instance—that the political principles according to which an absolutely competitive society is organized are taken to be the only conceivable ones. It is against this that I wish to argue.

But even if there are no contradictory interests or contradictory classes, there will always be differences of opinion. There will never be total unanimity, even in a communal society.

In such a society what might be called free intellectual life would not present itself as a problem. It would be taken for granted. The free development of individuality and of individual differences would flourish on the basis of a fundamental solidarity. The present, necessary emphasis on pluralism arises in a context where the economic powers of capital concentration and consumer regimentation fundamentally work in the opposite direction. When I consider how little use West Germans make of the formal possibilities that exist, I would say that people in the GDR use their head much more in political matters.

Yes, but they can do less than here. They have less possibility of influencing politics, the government or the society. They are powerless.

I'm not so certain how that will work itself out in the long term. It's certainly true now, and yet it is a rather strange contradiction. If I had written a book similar to *The Alternative* that dealt critically with the situation in West Germany, it would never have had the same effect here as *The Alternative* does over there.

That remains to be seen. The fact is that political freedoms and possibilities are much greater in bourgeois society than in the countries of actually existing socialism.

I don't disagree with that at all. But can you imagine the trade unions here coming as close to a political overthrow as Poland's Solidarity? That was truly an amazing story. Of course it doesn't negate the advantages of the political form here. I only want to point out how relative these things appear from the standpoint of a historical epoch. In a certain respect the greater indirect control here is more effectively repressive than the direct control over there.

7
Germany in the New Cold War

Let us turn to another problem that came up in the election campaign: the German question. If we understand by this the question of German unity, and of the relationship between developments in the two states, it is not altogether clear why it has emerged once again. What is the link between the German question and the eco-pacifist movement?

I said last autumn, and it has been published somewhere, that I had a positive attitude towards the perspective of German reunification. I should like to make it clear from the beginning that what I actually said then was not just a tactically misguided overstatement but a basically wrong judgement. Nevertheless, it should be understood in connection with my idea that the two German states are themselves too big, that we need a federation of provinces which territorially goes back beyond the Bismarck period to the time of the small German states, without, of course, their feudal structure. As I put it then, the localities should be stronger than the region, the region stronger than the province, and the province stronger than the federation. Although I would formulate my view differently now, my thinking at the time was that this national factor should give an added impetus to the issues of disarmament and ecology; that the Germans had something to contribute to the questions of peace, disarmament and detente; and that this national component could play an additional positive role.

Another factor was my own personal history. At the memorial celebration for Robert Havemann last year I read a poem by Johannes R. Becher on reunification which he wrote in 1952. I wrote my dissertation in the GDR on Johannes R. Becher, the title of which was 'The relationship between the German working class and the national question'. For Becher the questions of peace and reunification were inseparable.

I was very unhappy when, at the end of the Ulbricht period, the GDR finally gave up its national claim. At that time I still saw the question in terms of a socialist Germany, and I saw this surrender as a declaration of bankruptcy. Ulbricht, right up to the end, wanted to win the economic competition with West Germany, and one of the reasons for his fall was his continued insistence that the Soviet Union should invest in the GDR in order to bring this about. But Honecker put this off. The first task, he said, was to strengthen the socialist camp as far as Vladivostock and only then, by this route, to raise the German question again. Honecker was a realist and in 1970 nobody had the illusion that they could catch up with or overtake capitalism. So he quite consistently declared the division of Germany to be final. I saw that at the time as weakness. So this past history played a role in determining my attitude when the question was raised last autumn.

Another factor was my knowledge that many people in the SED were dependent on the link with West Germany: not in the sense of some rich uncle, but because the relation between the two Germanies gives the GDR a certain weight in its relations with Moscow. In every issue which comes up in the GDR, economic, political or strategic, its likely effect on the relationship with West Germany always plays an important role.

Now the Greens are a new element in the situation. Thus, after the initial panic reaction in arresting Petra Kelly, Gert Bastian and others on the Alexanderplatz, the East Berlin authorities soon realized what was happening and began to apologize. The next day, a letter arrived from Honecker, personally addressed to our people, thanking them for the visit and saying that he was willing to make the GDR a nuclear-free zone. He completely ignored their action on Alexanderplatz, which had certainly been an annoyance that he did not wish to see happen again. Then our letter to Honecker and his reply were published in place of the lead article in *Neues Deutschland*. Honecker, then, really does seem interested in the development of the Greens here. But, as I saw very early, there is an all-German dynamic to the Greens. The peace movements here and there have essentially the same character, and the Greens have a specific weight to bring to this whole question. That's probably why I went as far as I did in my formulation last autumn. We'll have to see what the population in both states say about this, whether they want a Federation of Eco-republics.

Before we begin to discuss the German Federation of Eco-republics, let us talk about a more immediate possibility: a neutral Germany.

The first thing to discuss is why the German question has again become so acute. Versailles contained the seeds of the Second World War in that it promoted the Nazi, imperialist mobilization. Later, the formation of the military blocs and the establishment of the Iron Curtain was meant to stabilize the peace in Europe. But the logic of the development of weapons technology, combined with the weakening of the hegemony of both superpowers, has made this military confrontation, with the inter-German border at its centre, into an unstable process. The question of Yalta is therefore not a CDU issue; it is our issue. The experience of 75 years of the German Reich was not a good one, but the present border is an external imposition and the people of Germany has never been given the opportunity to express its approval. That's why, when Germans go to Paris and say 'No reunification', nobody believes it. The present situation in Europe demands that the whole question of reunification be discussed again. The central point, however, is not reunification but the fact that this division of Germany was never democratically decided by the German people. The whole orientation towards reunification is in fact false.

The core of the matter is not the border itself but the military danger that it represents. Here on the Elbe the victors of the Second World War compete for world domination. In principle, the peace movement is bound to raise the question of nuclear disarmament on both sides, the greatest possible demilitarization on both sides, the withdrawal of American and Russian forces and so on. The German peace movement has the right to articulate its demands just as the Dutch movement does—'Disarmament East and West', 'Let's begin in Germany'. And there are good reasons for this, because it is precisely here in Germany that the bloc confrontation is most acute. It was no accident that the discussion of a pact-free policy, containing the perspective of reunification, began in Berlin.

How do you see the role of a neutral Germany, or two neutral German states, in the bloc system?

Before this discussion of the German question began, some of us had drawn up a charter for a nuclear-free Europe. A solution for Germany alone is not likely. The only thing we Germans can do, East and West, is pose the question for our own country. What we need in Germany is a government which, for the sake of peace and disarmament, risks going it alone. Of course, in the world of Realpolitik the German Government would never withdraw so far from the Western power system without some concession from the other side, without some new arrangement within the European political framework. In any case we are thinking not so much on the level of government as on the level of the popular movement. We want to take advantage of the specific contribution which Germans can make as a result of the particularly dramatic situation in Germany and the dynamic that has developed between the two German states. When you look at the opposition in Hungary in 1956, in Czechoslovakia in 1968 and now in Poland, and compare that with what exists in the GDR, you will see that this non-antagonistic eco-pacifist movement, which is not simply seeking a confrontation with Honecker, is much more a German than an Eastern-bloc opposition. The identity of this youthful, deeply-rooted opposition in both German states demonstrates that, beyond the Federal Republic and the GDR, there is still Germany. In spite of our small size, we must begin to work now as a serious candidate for political hegemony in this country. Our task is to accomplish a new structuring of the totality of political life, or at least to be the specific factor in this restructuring. And if the same movement exists in East Germany, the national factor cannot be avoided. It is part of reality itself.

What is your assessment of the peace movement in the GDR? It seems to be a very limited phenomenon.

Jena is the tip of the iceberg. When the State Security forcibly deported Roland Jahn, this was a sign of weakness, of failure to achieve its purpose by political means. I think that this indestructible network, existing throughout the GDR, is the expression of the younger generation there. The situation in the GDR, in spite of the distances and the loose organization, has created a very intensive movement. When those people there congregate with Eppelman in the Holy Saviour Church in East Berlin on 3 July, the intensity will be much greater than anything we could achieve at a similar peace meeting here. It is impossible to overestimate the effect of this on political cadres in the GDR, especially on the party intelligentsia.

In Hungary, Czechoslovakia and then Poland, the reform-communist tendency gradually disintegrated. Kadarization just succeeded in Hungary. In Czechoslovakia the reformists organized themselves in the Party but eventually met with failure. In Poland Kania and Rakowski, who may have wanted to attempt something like this, were incapable of putting a social platform together. In Czechoslovakia Charter 77 was a sign that the character of the opposition had gradually shifted towards issues of democratic rights. It would be a mistake to characterize this as a liberal or rightward move, and Hegedüs is correct when he calls it populist. In the GDR reform communism was never more than an intellectual or ideological trend without representation at the political level, and the people involved never left the party because there was no opportunity to do so. In spite of the fact that there's a great deal of Prussian authoritarianism among GDR party intellectuals, much more so than here or in Czechoslovakia, more than half of the party intelligentsia there would have opted for reform communism. But it became an ever more hopeless prospect.

The Soviet Union has specific reasons for wanting to hold on to East Germany and, in view of the proximity of NATO and West Germany, would never allow any experiment in the GDR unless it were an absolutely safe manoeuvre. So an opposition there has no possibility of crystallizing. And now, before reform communism has had its hour, a new movement is developing which has culturally been very much influenced by the West since 1968. There is an ideological interaction between those new types in the peace movement and the party intellectuals who realize there is no longer any prospect for reform communism. Then on top of all this come the Greens. The two German states are defined in relation to each other. The CDU needs the SED and the SED needs the CDU. Conditions in the GDR are the propaganda kit of the USA and vice versa. That's why, for the GDR, Willi Brandt was already a problem. So now when the Greens want to get rid of NATO, that changes the whole situation for the GDR. The SED leadership can't simply explain away the Greens as part of the power complex in the West.

But the Greens haven't changed very much in the GDR. The origins of the peace movement there are quite different.

The problem is that whereas Poland and Czechoslovakia—maybe not so much Hungary—are kept in the Eastern bloc militarily, there is a kind of negative consensus in the GDR that nothing can be changed, that, after all, the Nazi past and the American presence next door give the Russians some right to be there. But when we come out in favour of leaving NATO and creating a neutral Germany, the GDR leadership cannot dismiss us as part of the Western bloc. Petra Kelly goes over to Alexanderplatz and gets a thank-you letter from Honecker. And yet the peace people over there, people like Roland Jahn, are saying the same things as Petra Kelly. So what does Honecker have against them? Where's the legitimacy of his action?

The question is whether in reality the activity of the Greens in West Germany opens up a political space for the opposition in the GDR.

It is an inner space that's being opened there. During the Novotný period in Czechoslovakia, just before 1968, who could have imagined that within three months the majority of the Party would mobilize behind the reform course? A new crystallization of relations in the GDR depends on some new possibility in Europe as a whole, which in turn depends on the political processes within both blocs, not just in Germany. We want to achieve a conception of defensive defence, such that Russia no longer feels threatened by a militarized West Germany integrated into NATO, a militarized Western Europe allied with America, and such that the mutual hostility and distrust begin to break down. Perhaps this would come as a result of a West Germany hegemonized by the Greens. They could criticize the Greens ideologically as much as they wanted; it wouldn't matter any more.

The young generations on the two sides of the border are closer to each other than anyone else in Germany today, whether they realize it or not. We did not need an interpreter when we talked with Roland Jahn. The socialized individual both here and there displays the same hostility to the system, the same pacifist, non-violent tendency within this hostility. Realizing that the military apparatuses of the super-powers cannot be overthrown by violence, they make a virtue of necessity. It's not, of course, that the Germans have now suddenly become good, as once they were bad. This socialization process has world-historical causes.

Two fears about Germany are often expressed in the Western peace movement. One has rightist implications and is exemplified by André Gorz's belief that West German neutrality would weaken the West and strengthen Soviet influence both East and West. The second fear, expressed in England and France, is that in the final analysis a neutral Germany would become a nuclear Germany.

I have reached a better understanding with Gorz since my exchange with him in 1981–82.* But the second argument annoys me much more, because it suggests that the German peace movement should not be fully mobilized. If we refuse, out of respect for NATO, to pose the question of neutrality, then we would be setting ourselves here and now against the direction of history. German sovereignty has not existed since 1945, as a result of which Germany is merely the show-piece of the two blocs. And when the younger generation in Germany opposes this now, they do so not for altruistic reasons but because they perceive that their own vital interests are at stake. We can be happy that the peace movement is linked up with a movement for an alternative life-style, that it has nothing to do with the old Germany. If the peace movement in other countries wants to question our right to self-determination, especially given the key role of Germany in relations between the blocs, then I must say that they are

---

* The polemical exchange to which Bahro refers was translated in a special issue of *Telos* devoted to the European peace movements. See *Telos*, No. 51, Spring 1982.

not serious. This is a cowardly and faint-hearted political conception, and I can only say that we will ignore it.

Within Germany, and within the Green movement itself, we have many people—in Hamburg, for instance—who would nevertheless identify with this argument: not because of NATO but because they believe that, in the final analysis, German neutrality would strengthen the whole power complex. They are against NATO but are still afraid of the Germans. I wouldn't say that this fear is totally unfounded. Although there is no right-wing movement as such, a right-wing sentiment still exists. However, the whole approach is cowardly in relation to the overall European situation if we let the fear of Germany interfere with the necessary solution on a global scale.

My own view is that we must take the bull by the horns: we can't overcome the arms race and the structures that underlie the arms race, and still keep NATO. This is not to say that the present relationship of forces allows us to call for immediate withdrawal from NATO. The perspective of the eco-peace movement is to make the Potsdam foundation of the bloc conflict superfluous. If we achieve this goal, not just at the level of politics but at the level of psychic structure, thereby reversing the relationship between the authoritarian and the liberal in the German character, we could be close to the final settling of accounts with Germany's past. The material expression of this would be disarmament, or at least a turn towards defensive defence, and the withdrawal of the Americans. The next step would be for the Soviet Union to release Eastern Europe.

What, then, is the relation of forces in Germany? Is there a danger from the right? How can we help? Those are questions that need to be asked but have never yet been put to us. I must say that we can give no guarantees that it is we who are going to win. But what alternative is there? The way things are going now, Europe could be destroyed very quickly. At least we offer a chance; what we need from England and France and Italy is some trust. Of course our chances would be even better if the French Left did not support Strauss's foreign policy. What Gorz's position represents is a lack of understanding on the part of the French political milieu for the politics of social movements, a kind of neurotic processing of its own political tradition. It has to do partly with 1940, partly with its former identification with the Soviet Union, and partly with the desire to be fair or, as Gorz put it, to be more anti-Soviet than the Right. No one is more anti-Soviet than the French Left. Historically they have not understood the Russian Revolution as a counter-attack against the metropolis. They still see the French Revolution as *the* model of emancipation, in spite of the fact that it was very European and must be understood in the context of a self-destructive colonialism. With a few exceptions, the whole French intelligentsia is unwilling to recognize this.

Are you saying that the French don't understand Germany or that they want to impose a European idea on the whole world?

You could say that England was doomed by its being the motherland of industry, and France by its being the prototype of the European nation-state. France has always understood itself as the cultural heart of Europe, the *non plus ultra* of civilization. Germany and France have always competed for hegemony and the absolutism of both political styles is somehow related. The foundation of the German national state was a reaction to France. And the French—well, one needs an enemy, I suppose.

The most recent development in the West German eco-pacifist movement is a debate about the relation between the grass-roots movement and the level of state politics and diplomacy. One view is that we can discuss confederation or whatever we wish but that our main orientation has to be the grass-roots movement; in other words, our main task has to be to make the bloc border which runs through Germany pervious to the dialogue of the grass-roots movements on both sides, without carrying this to the level of state politics. Take the example of the Greens' action on Alexanderplatz. The Hamburg group thought that it played into the hands of Franz-Josef Strauss, who had been exploiting the death of a West German at a border-control station to step up tension between the two Germanies. In my view, we have to cut through this tendency to subordinate our politics to whatever kind of game the big powers are playing, to put off indefinitely the explicit struggle for hegemony. What Petra and the others did in East Berlin had nothing to do with Strauss, or the West German Government. When we go over to East Berlin and unroll our banner, that has nothing to do with what the CDU and the

SPD celebrate on 17 June, the day of German Unity. It is a defect of a section of the Left here, and also a section of the Greens, that they always assume our actions will play into the hands of the movement around the Day of German Unity.

Our task is to foster dialogue as a means of creating the most favourable conditions for the peace movement on the other side. If the SED is forced to react positively to us, then this creates greater space for the peace movement over there. Bastian must be of some value to them—otherwise they wouldn't have apologized. We must take advantage of this and of every hesitation in the authorities' attitude towards the independent peace movement. In Jena, where it got too hot, they cleared them out of the country. But they haven't stopped the action planned for 3 July in East Berlin. In practice they will be unable to destroy the network built up in the GDR, although much depends on the actions on both sides. In spite of Strauss and the CDU, we must maintain our refusal to recognize the border in practice.

It seems to me very important that when our parliamentary fraction invited Roland Jahn to a meeting on 17 June attended by members of the Hamburg group, we did not discuss from the point of view of hostility towards the other German state. At one level, then, we can exchange opinions with Honecker, explain what we want and find out what he wants. At another level we can exchange practical information, comparing, for instance, methods of dealing with the destruction of the forests. But this level of state politics is a goal for much later. We don't want to spread the illusion that a Kohl or Honecker government could ever bring about a German Con-federation. That would be to fly paper doves.

This will be much more difficult when the missiles are stationed in West Germany and the Soviets put something similar in the GDR.

Yes. That will probably come, and we must prepare ourselves now so that we don't give up our perspective and fall into despair. If the Pershings can be brought here, they can obviously be taken away again, but our task will be to make people even more aware of such likely consequences as the stationing of medium-range missiles in the GDR. Rearmament provokes even more rearmament and the whole situation becomes even more dangerous. However, the arms race cannot be turned around simply because something new isn't installed. There has to be an actual reduction. It is the beauty of the Russell Appeal that it is a long-term conception aimed at turning back the arms race—a completely different conception from that of the pro-Soviet DKP, which argues only against rearmament and gets caught up in the argument about who armed first. You can't win like that. We have to argue that even if the Russians double their number of SS20s, we still don't gain anything by installing new missiles here.

Do you think that an intermediate agreement is possible?

An intermediate agreement, with fewer Pershings or Cruise, would be an essentially cosmetic operation. The only important victory for the peace movement would be a decision to cancel deployment.

It would also mean that there would be no new weapons stationed in Germany.

Yes. Even Kohl would like that, because it would come about under his government. But I fear it won't happen. From the way Reagan and Weinberger are handling the Geneva negotiations, it is clear they don't intend to go back on their plan.

A recent book by Franz Alt, which is very successful here in Germany, strikes me as an important indicator. Alt is a TV interviewer and member of the CDU who, from a conservative standpoint, basing himself on the Sermon on the Mount, morally rejects the rearmament option. He also points to the identity of the arguments used on both sides. Now, whereas the peace movement involves a minority of committed people and the Greens can count on two million votes and a large number of sympathizers in the unions and the SPD, there are many people who would accept from Alt what they would never accept from us. We will win through when about half of the people who voted for Kohl, and want to keep him there for economic reasons, make it clear that nevertheless they didn't vote for the missiles. This is the significance of the peace-canvas strategy now being discussed by the Greens. Of course it's only a consultation, not a referendum, because the Greens also have the good old traditional distrust of the German character. But it is meant to give to those people who do not want the missiles here the opportunity to make their view known. In this way it would become clear to Kohl and the world at large that the majority of the German people doesn't want the missiles.

The nature of this bloc confrontation is often discussed in the peace movement and there is a tendency among certain people to deny that there is a real confrontation at all. The cold war, we are told, is a myth used to paper over the contradictions within each bloc. What do you think?

There's a host of arguments to support this analysis, which is particularly convincing in the case of the Soviet Union. The elites in both systems can best legitimate their position vis-à-vis their internal competitors by maintaining the situation that put them where they are. I agree with the argument that the bloc confrontation is used as a factor for internal stability. But I would also say that from the economic point of view the West no longer has any need to change the political structure of the Soviet Union. The world market has been re-created. The autonomy of the socialist system is very relative. The material structures, at the technological level, are generally the same. The technological inferiority of the socialist countries forces them on to the world market, subordinating them to the rules of that market which work against their interests, as in the case of the pipeline. There is no longer any political or military reason to change the regimes in Eastern Europe for the sake of profit.

I think you're exaggerating. It's true that there are economic contacts and that both sides profit from them. But the possibilities for the United States to influence or control the Soviet economy are not great, although they do attempt to do that in order to bring about a political change there. In reality the Soviet economy is rather autonomous, not completely but to a great extent.

I think you overestimate this. Of course it's only in an indirect manner that the world market and the arms race exert their sway over

Gosplan, determining and distorting the economic structure of the Soviet Union. Nevertheless, in order to keep up with the West, including in the arms race, the Soviet Union is forced to import Western technology and therefore to sell its raw materials cheaply—and then there is the unsolved problem of agriculture. In short, the Soviet economic profile is a variable within the productive forces of a world market controlled by capital. If we put in perspective all the other factors, social, political and cultural, it is actually the nuclear bomb which allows the Soviet Union to play the role of second superpower. And yet, this very superpower role is fatally overburdening the Soviet economy: the economic competition with capitalism which the Russian Revolution initiated has been a failure. For economic purposes, then, it is unnecessary for the West to change the structures of political power in Eastern Europe. Of course if they didn't exist, the rate of profit might be higher. But the resources and the economy of Eastern Europe are already integrated into the business cycle, and what is not integrated is residual. The mechanisms of arms competition and technological dependence are so powerful that the Soviet Union is more or less a periphery of the world market.

But in spite of that, there's confrontation between the blocs.

Yes. When I say 'periphery of the world market', I am within the problematic not of socialism but of colonialism, not of a socialist but of an anti-colonialist response to the capitalist system. The challenge to the West represented by the existence of the Soviet Union was and is a political challenge. Lenin's conception of the general crisis of capitalism indicated the same thing: that it is not the profit of any particular branch of capital but the total system which is at stake. That crisis appears today as a struggle for world domination, but it is not a struggle between two systems, capitalist and socialist. I characterize it negatively as the non-capitalist road to industrial society, which is simply another name for a particular type of development. The main point is that the underdeveloped countries want to push forward along the central axis of the developed countries.

There are in fact only two worlds: the expansive European civilization (in which I include America, Australia, Canada, Japan) and the other. At the very beginning of the century Lenin followed this development very astutely, in Turkey, Persia and Asia. He foresaw the revolutions in Asia, and Russia was simply the forerunner of this kind of response of the underdeveloped world to the challenge of the capitalist metropolitan type of production, a response in the final analysis to the ability of the capitalist centre to destroy those other civilizations right to the core of their cultural identity. The instrument of this destruction was not the cannon but technology. The response, however, was still determined from the centre. It is no accident that the Soviet Union suffers most from the arms race. This counter-development, which leads to military confrontation, will not provide the breakthrough and is in fact counter-productive for those involved. The response to European expansion cannot be counter-expansion but a cultural transformation, in the periphery as well as in the centre. Such a cultural revolution would revolutionize the social-psychic model through which human development has come to mean material expansion and military conflict over fewer and fewer resources. The social problem of inequality in the nineteenth century was still contained within a national context that prevented social explosion, but today we are threatened by a world-scale explosion. When this social contradiction combines with national and racial struggles, the road to catastrophe comes into view. This is the origin of the missiles. If you examine the ideologies of East and West, you will find that this conflict is without real substance. The military confrontation has acquired its own independence.

That's also E.P. Thompson's explanation.

Yes. This level of explanation is very important, because the East-West conflict, in itself, is without substance. But I do think that it is anchored in something deeper. In fact, since 1917 this East-West conflict has actually been the forward thrust of the North-South conflict.

But would that have been the case if the German Revolution had succeeded? Doesn't this contradiction exist within the developed countries themselves?

I doubt more and more that this is the case. Comrades in the GDR have had endless discussions with me about the reasons for the failure of the German revolution. I really don't think it is to be explained by some subjective factor: that the Party was founded too late, that it didn't have the right leader, that it had left-wing and right-wing deviations, and so on. I have come to the conclusion that the lower classes of the imperialist metropolis cannot make a revolution. Marx was fundamentally wrong in assuming that the problems of humanity would be solved by working-class revolution in the most developed capitalist countries. Rather, those were right who said very early on that the working classes were imperialist.

Those are two different things: one that they aren't revolutionary, the other that they're imperialist. They may profit from imperialism, but whether, in any political sense, they are imperialist is quite another matter.

That depends on your concept of imperialism. Of course they are not imperialist in the terms of Lenin's definition. But, for me their role as fellow-colonialists makes them both imperialist and non-revolutionary. The lower classes in Greece always had their class differences with the oligarchy, with the Polis. Yet there was always a political consensus that Athens should remain the spider in the web. The class opposition was always relative and subordinate to the shared interest that the cake in Athens should be as big as possible. It was the same in Rome and it has become the same again now in Europe.

There was a time when the world market wasn't a daily reality around the globe, when attention could be given to the internal contradictions within Europe itself. That is why the Paris Commune was possible. However, it is now a simple fact, and not a moral criticism, that workers in the metropolis have become the companions or fellow-travellers of capital. The socialist motivation of the Russian Revolution was an illusion. It wanted to be a contribution to the proletarian revolution in the centre, but the October revolution didn't develop in that direction. I don't want to say there was absolutely no foundation for this illusion—after all, the proletariat and bourgeoisie did exist also in Russia. Nor am I suggesting that there isn't a proletarian-bourgeois problem in the world today. What I am arguing is that we have taken our image of the conflict between wage-labour and capital and blown it up into a world image. Many people on the Left, and also in the Greens, see the East-West conflict merely as an expression of the conflict between wage-labour and capital. When the Trotskyists talk of the workers' state, for example, they present the conflict between wage-labour and capital as the pivotal contradiction of history which Russia simply reproduces at the level of the state. This whole concept is false to the core, as was Marx's belief that the proletarian revolution in England would be the salvation of India. The class-struggle factor certainly exists, but it is not the dominant one. The compulsion that lay on Peter the Great to modernize Russia is the secret truth of the October revolution. By 1917 the totality of its culture and civilization was being threatened, and the old elite had proven itself incapable of meeting this challenge. The people had no choice but to revolt. The Russian revolution was a change of elites, and it was the same in China. These were anti-colonial revolutions in which the real issue was metropolis and periphery. The real meaning of the East-West conflict does not reveal itself on the inter-German border, but it was very clearly revealed when Andropov was here in Germany and said in answer to a *Spiegel* interviewer's question about Afghanistan that the Americans were not prepared to let themselves be pushed around in Nicaragua. The real conflict, we could almost say, is black–white.

Although Afghanistan and Nicaragua are said to be the 'back gardens' of the major powers, it is a fact that the Americans are trying to prop up a very reactionary class structure and society in their back garden. The Russians have made many mistakes in Afghanistan, but at least they are trying to transform that feudal society. Even if they are both gardeners, they are doing very different things in their gardens.

I consider the Russians intervention in Afghanistan to be just as bad. But that's not my point. The barbarity of industrialization and the politics of modernization are destroying the cultural identity of most peoples in the Third World. In that sense the Russians in

Afghanistan are simply the agents of the world market. What the Kabul elite always wanted was to institute a Mercedes culture in its capital city. This is the basic text they get from the West, and Moscow is the agency for it even in Soviet Asia.

In the case of a country where the majority of the people have no medical care, where a quarter of the children die in their first year, where illiteracy is ninety per cent and so on, it is not our task to defend the national tradition. Development for Afghanistan means health, education, emancipation of women. Whether the Russians should do that is another question. But I have no doubt that this kind of development is positive: it would be irresponsible romanticism to defend the other tradition of poverty, superstition and backwardness.

I don't see it that way.

Do you want a quarter of the children in Afghanistan to die in their first year? Is that the national tradition you want to defend?

No. The point is not to defend such a tradition, but that the solution to the problems of the people of Afghanistan is taking the form of a foreign imposition. The whole of the country's previous development presupposed a certain international constellation. In fact, Third World poverty is a consequence of capitalist industrial development. The equilibrium in those societies has been destroyed by a historical process originating in Europe, one of whose agents in Asia has been the Soviet Union. It's not a question of guilt, but of the historical extension of this industrial monoculture to the whole world. And it is false to think that the challenge represented by poverty, mortality and so on should be met in the way it is presently being met in Afghanistan, by the very forces who in the broadest historical sense were responsible for the situation in the first place. It is no accident that this has led to civil war. More important, however, is the fact that the conflicts in Central America and Afghanistan are also the real front of the East-West confrontation, which should in turn be seen as part of the North-South conflict. What is so terrible about the autonomy of this military confrontation is that everything else is subordinated to it. Even after 1945 the real front in the East-West conflict wasn't in Europe. MacArthur was right when he said that the real front was against communism in Asia, in other words against Korea and Vietnam. We have now reached the point where this European expansionism will become a living nightmare.

The question of wage-labour and capital in the centre is the same as the question of centre and periphery on a world scale. Both must be overcome in their totality. The problems of history need a new type of resolution, and we are offering a new, untried perspective for the way-out from capitalism. The other way was tried here in the centre and it failed. Capitalism is a world system articulating metropolis and periphery, and it is at this level that the solution must be found.

8

From Red to Green: Industrialism and Cultural Revolution

What you have been saying raises a number of questions concerning relations between the developed and underdeveloped countries. Your critique of industrialism may sound plausible in Germany or some other rich country, but not in a poor country. For the under-developed countries the only way out of poverty is more trade with the richer nations, more industry. But your programme is against this. Isn't it undemocratic in as much as it condemns the poorer countries to continued poverty?

An African writer has written a book whose title I like very much: *Poverty: the Wealth of the People.* He draws a distinction between poverty and misery (*Armut* and *Elend*). All the things you have raised, the model you have described for overcoming poverty, would send the peoples of the Third World into a tunnel without an exit, because the living standard they are aiming for is no longer achievable. In 1800 or 1830, the period about which Engels wrote, the working classes of Europe still had the prospect of a bourgeois way of life—indeed, they were able to achieve something of that order because of the existence of the periphery. But for the present periphery there is no further periphery to be exploited, no way of attaining the good life of London, Paris or Washington.

As long as this model still exists at the centre, my argument can only be an ideology for the people of the underdeveloped countries. In a sense, the commune perspective I advocate for the developed countries would involve us in becoming something like the Third World. Otherwise, the imposition of our model on the Third World will just lead to the kind of situation I saw in Mexico—first, people move to the shanty-town on the edge of the city, then the next generation can buy a run-down car, trying to reproduce what exists in the metropolis. For its part, Eastern Europe is nothing but third-class industrialization. Czechoslovakia and the GDR are second-class because they were half-capitalist before, but the Soviet Union is definitely third-class from the point of view of its success for the masses. This is a hopeless perspective: it won't work because the limits have already been reached.

Do you mean the physical limits of nature, or moral and political limits?

These belong together more than the 'or' in your question would imply.

I'm not convinced that it is impossible for the four and a half billion people in the world to reach the living standard of West Germany. Whether that's desirable is another matter, but I don't see that it's impossible.

It is possible for a historical minute, but then ten billion humans are dependent on it. They will become part of the industrial mill and be unable to turn back. I believe that human evolution began to go wrong with the English industrial revolution.

In what way?

I see exterminism as rooted in industrialism.

You say that in the past two thousand years nothing good has been achieved?

I didn't say that and I wouldn't say it.

So you concede that there has been progress?

I don't think of it in this way. If in the whole historical process of civilization, especially of European civilization, the destructive tendency clearly wins the upper hand, if we're heading for self-destruction, then we are dealing with a sickness of the totality. It is clearly wrong to try to divide it up between the good achievements and the bad. They are part of the same totality which has to be questioned, not in the sense that I don't want the most modern medicine, but in the sense that none of the achievements removes the need to question the whole structure. On the whole the European culture of the past two or three thousand years, which announced its birth in the *Iliad*, has been exterminist in its most inner dispositions, modelling itself on individual competition and the Olympia principle of 'more, higher, faster, better'. These dispositions have in the recent period led to capitalism; they were its precondition.

Are you not harking back to the Stone Age? It may sound provocative, but that's how your position will be understood.

Take the microchip. Its benefits are easy enough to imagine, but as long as this whole system is constituted as it is—and I don't mean merely its more recent capitalist characteristics—then the microchip will only serve big brother.

I haven't noticed in history that non-Europeans have been all that pacifist. Aggression and the use of force are to be found everywhere in history. I agree that industrialism has increased the possibilities of destruction, but from a moral or psychological or anthropological point of view, aggression in history has been a world-wide phenomenon.

I have also looked into the anthropological basis for all this and tried to determine whether the European way is an accidental specialization in the human species or whether it is a specialization which, as so often happens in evolution, will lead to the destruction of the species if it continues unbroken. We must see whether in the nature of the species there is the possibility of a more favourable specialization, one which gives the species a future. If this happens, or to express it perhaps more succinctly, if a community such as that which Francis of Assisi wanted to establish were to use the microchip, I wouldn't see any problem in that.

The concept of 'exterminism' which you have developed in your work is very complex and seems to have four different senses. The first, initially proposed by E.P. Thompson and others, has to do with the arms race and the tendency to nuclear war. The second is concerned with mass starvation in the Third World—the daily exterminism lived now by hundreds of millions. The third refers to the destruction of nature as a result of the continuation of industrialism, which could, ecologists argue, destroy our natural habitat. These are three historically specific aspects, peculiar to the contemporary epoch. But there is also a fourth meaning, and this is the psychological and anthropological element of power in the human psychology which, you argue, is exterminist and which, if it has a history, is thousands of years old. The use of 'exterminism' in your writings seems to confuse these four ideas, each of which is questionable in itself. But one can also ask if a campaign against exterminism in the first three senses can be combined with a campaign against exterminism in the fourth sense. A strategy for the psychological transformation of humanity, for a complete moral transformation, for psychological therapy, is perhaps compatible at the level of analysis with a campaign against the bomb. But when you come to the level of politics, isn't there a danger that the campaign against the bomb and mass starvation will lose itself in the campaign for a 'new birth', for mass therapy, and so on? Are you not engaged in a utopian dilution of the historically specific drive against the bomb?

I could put a different question to you. Doesn't the struggle against militarism since the eighties of the last century teach us that campaigns against the bomb, *as* campaigns against the bomb, are not winnable? It seems to me that without a cultural revolution we have no chance against the arms race. We may have a temporary success against a single weapons system, but the foundations deep in the European soil are warlike, especially in North west Europe, and then comes the additional fact that we can't maintain our living standard without a Rapid Deployment Force. This Rapid Deployment Force is part of the consensus. Popular support for the intervention in Iran was so easily obtained because people felt threatened in their cultural identity. That's the psychology we're dealing with. People voted Kohl because they wanted to keep up their living standard.

They were well aware that he would also bring the missiles, but that was a third-rate question for them. They don't basically question the defence of the free West.

You see exterminism as something anchored in human psychology?

Yes. In fact I would fault Marx for not having been materialist enough, in that he undervalued three levels of reality which have their weight in a monistic conception. Marx took the level of objectification and on this basis built up a historical materialism. But this presupposes the level of reality which is objective spirit, at the summit of which is the fact that the human being possesses consciousness. Marx said himself that everything goes through the head. Beneath this is the level of human nature as a whole, and beneath this again is nature, from which we originate and which Marx regarded as somehow passive. In other words, his static model did not take sufficiently into account the impulses which brought forth the human being in the first place. I believe that the truth lies some where between this static model and the Aristotelian entelechy.

Now, when I speak of psychology, I am speaking of the quintessence of this process of development. This is where the psychodynamic, the sociodynamic begins. History is primarily psychodynamic. The theory of Engels in *The Role of Labour in the Transition from Ape to Man* is wrong because it places the accent in the wrong place.

In this context you speak of a Conversion, a Transformation or a Rebirth of humanity which has a spiritual or a religious aspect. You use the term 'conversion' in a secular sense to suggest a change of outlook. What exactly do you mean by that?

I see exterminism as a multidimensional phenomenon. The three things you mentioned are appearance only and explain nothing in themselves. Beneath those I see the industrial system with its technostructure and its science; beneath this the driving mechanism of capitalism; beneath this European cosmology, and beneath this the more general anthropological factors. In our campaign strategy we must begin from both poles. We need a defensive strategy which deals with the surface phenomena of exterminism more than with intermediate layers such as industrialism. This political strategy must win us space and time. But at the same time, we must begin at the other pole with a critique of human need, of human nature. The anthropologist Portman says that homo sapiens is born a year too soon and has an extra-uterine gestation year of total dependence on the mother. Then come another two or three years of complete social dependence, followed by quite a few years of being tied to the socialization process. In other words, there is a surplus of external determination against which a psychological revolution is bound to occur, in which knowledge is power-oriented both towards nature and towards the parents and community. Here I would share Wilhelm Reich's view of our character structure and knowledge structure as competitive and conflict-oriented, and of our expansion as a fleeing forwards. In my eyes, exemplary figures like Christ or Buddha sought the new man not by looking forwards, but by looking backwards or inwards—in other words, they divested themselves of the conditions which society imposed on them from birth. We have to find a way for all humans to make the breakthrough that Christ and Buddha made. The existence of Christ, or Buddha or Francis of Assisi, demonstrates that it is possible for humans to deal with the aggressive warlike quality they have as humans. Must it always be minorities that achieve this? Or is it possible for us to organize consciously towards this end? Without conscious organization, without institutionalization, it is not possible to achieve this.

A part of this transformation must deal with patriarchy, the inequality between man and woman. The women's movement has a place at both poles of your strategy, as an opponent of the bomb and of the deep structure of human domination. You have spoken of patriarchy as a ten-thousand-year-old substratum. What do you think are the possibilities for a transformation of patriarchy? And what is the role of women's emancipation in your perspective?

This concerns the oldest social conflict (along with the antagonism between different generations) and the deepest level of social transformation. The women's movement very strongly reflects the polarity we have talked about. There is a very counter-aggressive and combative political strategy which, though quite understandable, appears to be counter-productive. But the main contribution which the women's movement can make is at the other pole—that is, in the peaceful dissolution of this earliest crystallization of the power structure.

In a sense the transformation I envisage is also a reconstruction of God. The function of God in the Old Testament was always that of regulator. Marx called it the intellectualized species-being. Christ and Buddha never broke out of the framework of this patriarchal structure. Indeed, I see the Christian and Buddhist hostility to sensuality as a tribute to patriarchy. The logos is male.

Feminism, in one aspect, is the final consequence of bourgeois emancipation. This element, dating from the French Revolution, is justified but still lies *within* the logic of the civilization which has to be overcome. From the other pole, however, it is different. If the concept of a world-historical mission of the proletariat is not in fact true, then it is entirely possible that women have something like a general mission in this respect.

Although many of your ideas have changed since you wrote The Alternative, *and you are working now in a different society, is there not a basic consistency in your concept of emancipation as something cultural and psychological? There are similarities between your current idea of emancipation and the concept you developed in the final section of* The Alternative.

I still make use of the model of emancipation that I developed in chapters 10 and 11 of *The Alternative*. But although my commune perspective is somehow contained in the association model of that final section, there is an important difference. In essence my concept of emancipation was then still located within the framework of the Enlightenment, with its emphasis on the communal appropriation of the totality for the full development of individuality. Another element of continuity is the fact that in the highly non-pluralist society of the GDR, where my critical orientation was not rooted in some particular interest group, my experience and the deepest structures of my thinking led me to question the society as a whole, to dispute the totality, to conceptualize a new hegemony. I couldn't have thought otherwise. That was certainly an advantage when I came to the West, because I could never be satisfied with just a protest or opposition movement. The problem is not to create a space for minorities but to create a new solution for the whole of society. The runways are there for us in popular consciousness but they are, so to speak, blocked with rubbish. Our task is to clear away this rubbish. I had a conversation recently with Jorschke Fischer, a parliamentary delegate from Frankfurt, and our deepest disagreement was on the question of whether all people should have the capacity to communicate with God. He doesn't believe that. So in the final analysis one is left with manipulation, republicanism from above, Jacobinism. It may well be that plebiscitary politics is dangerous now because of the concrete relation of forces, but for *them* this is always the case.

How has your attitude to Marx changed since The Alternative? *You no longer appear to be a Marxist in any recognizable sense.*

From the standpoint of personal identity, it is completely different to be a Marxist in the West and in Eastern Europe. In Eastern Europe it's like being a Christian in the Middle Ages: Marxism is the intellectual universe to which everything else relates. When I saw, for instance, that certain parts of Freud were not compatible with Marxism, my attitude was to regard that simply as a question of a subjective limitation of Marx which didn't alter the capacity of the Marxist conception to integrate whatever was correct in Freud. Marxism is not a distinctive position over there: what is distinctive is to be a heretical Marxist, Luther against the Pope. A particular identity is created in the East which is in fact minoritarian, unrepresentative of the whole. It is a party-limited universe since the majority of the population is not Marxist. The Party is to a certain extent an alien body. This was an important experience for me, and it gave me the impetus to break from it. How could I have an orientation towards the social whole and at the same time have the people against me?

As far as my reception here was concerned, Ernest Mandel, the main claimant to continuity with classical Marxism, saw *The Alternative* as an inadequate and half-successful attempt to reconstruct Marxism. But that was not my purpose. You will certainly find places in *The Alternative* where I claim to have correctly reconstructed Marx. But you misunderstand this if you don't see the difference between the position of Marxism in the East and in the West. The issue was not the development of theory but the reconstruction of the Gospel. I experienced no problem and didn't feel myself heretical when, in one of the middle chapters, I gave up the concept of the centrality of the working class. I acted exactly as I had done in the case of Freud. Reality had changed, Marx couldn't have seen it, Marxism had to be further developed to integrate this, and so on. But here in the West I find myself forced more and more often to say that I am no longer a Marxist. To be a Marxist here means to assent to the fact that a definite political-theoretical conception has been firmly established and still requires firm adherence. It is true that Marxism is a very specific conceptualization—if, that is, we take it to involve the centrality of the proletariat, the belief that the solution to the world's problems is to be found by means of the class struggle in the richer nations, the view that internal contradictions are more important than external ones, internal class struggles more central than the contradiction between culture and civilization. To the extent that those elements are essential to the conceptualization, I would say that I have left Marxism behind.

Part of the problem here is that the personal identity of so many on the Left is tied to a particular conception of what it means to be Marxist. This is not the case for me. I have no loyalty to a concept. I do not regard it as productive, for example, to enter into arguments with Trotskyists who say that here I deviate, there I deviate. Already in the GDR, where Marxism was the centre of my development for over twenty years, the dynamic of Marx's ideas had led me to new conclusions. There are many particular elements in Marx that I still find useful, but the structure itself I have abandoned. For me Marxism is a quarry. After the fall of the Roman Empire ordinary people used the stones of the fallen temples to build their homes and their churches. This is productive use of material. There are also structural elements that I use, even if I now refer to the formation as exterminism. My whole Marxist background has, of course, gone into this restructuring. In a certain respect you could characterize my thinking as a regression, not for reasons that are subjective, but because that is the determination of the objective situation itself. The class struggle is not the solution. The problem is the dissolution of the entire formation itself. From scientific socialism I have returned to utopian socialism, and politically I have moved from a class-dimensional to a populist orientation. My exemplar would be Thomas Münzer. There is a difference between Jesus and Christ. Jesus is human, Christ is the elevation to concept, and Münzer is on the level of Christ for me, the ideal type. Justice for him meant liberation for the peasantry to enable it to attain the freedom of the Christian, to communicate directly with God. The resolution of a social problem was not Münzer's ultimate intention. He wanted to resolve the problem of the liberation of the peasantry because equality before God was not achievable under its existing conditions. That's why I like the rainbow banner of the peasants, the peasants not as a class but as the people.

The 'Eternal Council' was set up in Mühlhausen. The political reality, however, was not at the abstract level of opposing class interests. It encompassed, as Thompson describes it in the case of the English working class in the eighteenth century, the whole of society. Marxist historians later drew out the class differences, but that was not the logic of the peasant war. Those factors may assume some importance now when we look back and try to discover the reasons for its failure. But the figure of Thomas Münzer represents for me the incarnation of the Ordine Nuovo.

The relation between Prophet and Politician is a problem for the Greens and for yourself. Of course a politician can have a vision, but the divide is always there when compromises have to be made, concrete programmes drawn up and so on. It is a real danger for you that the Greens could remain a minority, organized in separatist communes, withdrawn and marginalized from society. But you see that differently. You want to bring about change by engaging in politics on the one hand and starting to create a new society on the other. Yet your concept of 'liberated zones' in industrialized society is a profoundly ambivalent one.

I want to see the emphasis shifted from politics and the question of power towards the cultural level. It is the greatest merit of Gramsci that he managed to focus attention on the problematic of hegemony, although still ultimately with a view to power. With Gramsci it was still too direct. Not by accident was he in favour of Fordism. He saw the task, at the cultural level, as the transformation of everyone into workers and engineers within, of course, a wider horizon.

I believe that at the cultural-political level, the strategy of non-violence will win through, developing out of subjective necessity and providing a new foundation for politics. I'm not interested simply in parliamentary politics, and I want to shift the emphasis to the prophetic level in order to have a new determining influence on politics. For this problem of politics and prophecy Münzer is again the model. In a concrete situation politics can dominate, but our problem is to decide whether we want to invest ninety-nine per cent of our energy in the carousel of politics or only fifty per cent. Of course the Greens themselves, as a political party, are the arm of the movement, and I can't go to the parliamentary fraction and argue for less than fifty per cent politics. But my specific contribution is to try to shift the emphasis towards the other pole. I want to begin with the transformation of subjectivity, but directed towards a political goal. The task is not just to heal ourselves but to be aware that the movement has a healing mission.

What is your vision of the alternative society, of your utopia?

The logic and the tempo of expansionism, as it has existed up to now, have prevented the emergence of a natural order because they have always necessitated the encroachment of overriding regulation. The biological domain allows of no substitute for the equilibrium of the natural world. As long as we have this expansion, we will continue to have disproportionality, the encroachment of regulation and a competitive drive impelling the whole thing forward. In the absence of natural order communes have never survived. The American communards of the eighteenth and nineteenth centuries were the pioneers of this *homo occidentalis simplicissimus*.

I believe we have now reached the point where humanity has to find a new stable life-form in which its forward development is an inward journey rather than an external expansion. The problem is not the abolition of technology but its subordination. Our aim has to be the 'reconstruction of God'—in other words, the kind of regulation which can only come from the re-creation of spiritual equilibrium, within those levels of nature neglected by Marx where human consciousness comes into contact with the external world. This is the goal, then: a reproduction of social being in which the economy, and the technological component of the economy, are integrated elements. We must eat, dress, have free time and try to overcome the rigid division between economic reproduction and social communication. Utopia is the optimal satisfaction of basic human needs, not just physical but social. Human development requires a basic security, a sense of being sheltered by a community, where you don't have to think of your old-age pension at the age of twenty, where individuality can be expressed and enjoyed in communication with others, where self-realization can take place in a different sense from that of European individualism. This communication with the totality therefore points towards a social being compatible with human nature and with the limits set by the external world. The individual elements of this conception are not new and have been described by utopian socialists and communists for hundreds of years. Certain things are obvious: that a solution to problems is best found in small groups, that human companionship for the satisfaction of mutual need requires a certain minimum number, and that some access to the wider world must be possible. In the rules of the Benedictines, for instance, there is a section which deals with travelling for monks.

So you are not opposed to travelling? In your utopian world of ecological villages trade may not be important, but travel and communication will remain possibilities. Travel, you concede, is a cultural need.

Yes. But if it means that we have to see all the countries in the UN and to fly around the world twenty-seven times, then this is obviously not possible. I don't imagine the appropriation of our world in this way. There are natural limits. Perhaps it will be adequate if we travel to Italy twice, as Goethe did.

As I said earlier, we should also have informational communication around the whole world; only the material transport system must be massively reduced. Our problem now in Europe is not to go into detail about particular concepts of self-reliance that might work for the whole world. A great deal has already been written about that. What is needed is to take the initiative, so that people can come together and attempt communal life, with enough commitment not to run back to a job after a few weeks or so. If twenty people are sufficiently committed to a project, they can draw in two hundred more. This is big enough for a self-managing, self-caring social community. Here lies the key to institutional security for the experience of the self, what the Buddhists call Karma.

You have, in some of your previous works, written about the role of culture and in particular about Beethoven. What is the relation of this to your overall view?

The way in which the French Revolution formulated the problem of emancipation still stood within the context of individualist European culture. Rolland, for example, speaks of the time when one Christopher Columbus after another went out to conquer the world. In practice bourgeois emancipation has meant this republic of kings. There's a poem by Hölderlin, *The Oak*, in which at the top of every mountain stands god-like man. This republic of kings is actually a society of Indo-Germanic petty princes.

My Beethoven book, which I wrote between 1967 and 1969, was still entirely within this tradition. Even in *The Alternative* my concept of emancipation was not free from what, in the final analysis, is an expansionist image of self-realization. But in my final years in the GDR I already came to favour Mozart and Schubert. I was more open to their non-antagonist relation with the world, so distinct from the combative, overpowering orientation of Beethoven.

In an earlier discussion, you spoke about Solidarnosc and about whether this historical experience refuted the theses of The Alternative *on the role of the proletariat. Now, one and a half years after the military takeover, how do you see the situation in Poland with respect to the perspective contained in* The Alternative*?*

I am even more certain now that developments in Poland can only be understood within a populist political framework. Of course the situation in the factories did play an important role, but the political constellation there is not analogous to the conflict of labour and capital. Poland was on the brink of a struggle for power. What the society there needs is a new crystallization of its entire institutional system—a development which the Soviet Union must stop at any price. There is also an international aspect in Western Europe because of the relationship with America, but the European and American structures are so similar that this is not experienced as a foreign or alien imposition. The situations here and in Poland are similar only to the extent that people's interests in both cases require a radically new organization of social life and social institutions. That was the essence of what happened in Poland, and all forces outside the apparatus cooperated to bring this action together. That it crystallized around the trade union had to do with the fact that in Poland the dominant process has been one of industrialization. But although there is a working class in the broadest sense, this concept only confuses the real nature of the system.

The 'anti-Soviet' political element was decisive in Poland because the new institutionalization which the nation needed was against Soviet interests, as these are determined by the logic of bloc confrontation. The entire political question centred on the issue of national identity, and it was predetermined that the main protagonist had to be the institution which is the main guarantor of Polish national identity, the Church. You could almost say that Solidarnosc was an outpost of the Church, certainly at the level of ideology or hegemony. No conspiracy was involved. This is how it was in Poland. Industrialization is still relatively new and the cultural identity which stems from the peasant tradition is still unbroken. Even in the period in which Solidarnosc occupied the foreground, the perspective was not socialist in any traditional sense. It was typical that when Walesa visited Japan, he came back proclaiming the need to Japanize Poland. At the decisive level Walesa was no alternative to Gierek. Gierek wanted to build a new Poland—hence his investment programme. And when Walesa wanted to Japanize Poland, he had in mind that peculiar constellation of absolute subordination, that corporatist patriarchal model which fits so easily with Catholicism. Walesa was actually very representative of the popular movement, including what went on in the factories. I don't want to exclude the KOR or other factors, but Walesa and his advisers from the Episcopate constituted the mainstream of this process in Poland.

The Church, not the Party, is the only force in Poland with ideological control.

I doubt very much that there was any similarity with the West. I agree that the movement was not socialist in its ideology, programme or structure, but nor was it a movement against industrialism. On the contrary, it demanded more consumer goods and higher wages. In addition, there was a whole series of democratic and political problems. One could say that both the eco-pacifist movement in the West and Solidarnosc in Poland were protest movements against the political structure, but the reasons are rather different in the two cases. You cannot assimilate the Polish struggle to the ecological movement in the West.

In both cases, the structure is one of popular resistance and not of a class-against-class formation. We are dealing with a populist political construction, and it is at this level that I wanted to establish their similarity. When you take the GDR, the movements are in fact identical.

How do you see the perspectives for resistance in Eastern Europe in general? Which forces or tendencies could weaken Soviet domination? Are there tendencies with an effective emancipatory perspective?

The Polish movement was, and still is, very effective in as much as it was able to block any initiative by Moscow or the system in Eastern Europe. I don't see any chance of a solution favourable to the Soviet Union. The relation of forces in the country is such that the General could only gain some popular support as the Adjutant of the Virgin Mary, Queen of Poland.

It is an important point for us in the peace movement that even at the military level Solidarnosc paralysed the Soviet Union. Poland was a defeat for the Warsaw Pact, and we now have greater credibility here when we say the Russians are not about to march over Western Europe when they can't even deal with Poland. Moreover, any disarmament initiative here would clearly undermine the legitimacy of Russia's military hegemony over Eastern Europe and open up a perspective for a return of sovereignty to Eastern Europe on, let us say, the model of Finland. Poland means for me that Stalin's victory is historically finished, that the Soviet Union has already lost Eastern Europe, and that, with the possible exception of the GDR, it can only be retained militarily. The *cordon sanitaire* around the Soviet Union has become a hostile belt.

Did Solidarnosc have any impact in the GDR?

No. I would say rather that it had a stabilizing effect. The GDR leadership, which thinks in the long term, must have been immensely worried that, with no hinterland except for its unreliable Polish ally, it will have to survive on the direct link to Moscow. You must imagine what it was like in the fifties, when the saying used to be 'from the Elbe to the China Sea', to realize how incredibly insecure their perspective must be now. And this is another reason why the GDR leadership has such an interest in internal developments in West Germany at the present moment. It's their only hope. Moscow can keep them in power, but economically it has nothing new to offer.

In the short term, however, those small-scale Polish speculators who cleaned out the GDR shops from Dresden to Frankfurt-on-Oder did a lot to prevent the Polish disease from spreading in the GDR. The attitude of the East German worker was that the Poles ought to work. The danger was much greater inside the Party in 1968. Provincialism or national narrowness is an additional factor, since people in the GDR don't deal with such things at the analytic level of our present discussion. But it was enough for them to watch the papal visit on television and listen to the popular version of the national anthem ('Give us back our free Poland...') in order to realize which was the truly dominant force. This is all discussed in liberal Party circles, and when the SED leadership tightens the reins, they are already prepared for it. They are far from pleased, but they'll accept it because the consensus is there.

From my earlier reform-communist perspective, I didn't foresee the eco-pacifist movement that is now developing in the GDR. If I had foreseen it, I'm not at all sure I would have left. The opposition there now is not a political opposition against the Party; it is more of an intellectual opposition whose goal, as is the case with the eco-peace movement here, is ideological hegemony.

Is the movement there ecological or only pacifist?

The first book put together recently in the GDR and published over here is called *Concrete is Concrete*. It's the same movement. They too ride their bicycles against pollution, plant trees and so on.

You have said that, for the peace movement in the East, the tanks are more important than the missiles.

When Roland Jahn was here, he said that of course they were opposed to the Pershings, as was the GDR regime, but that they were also for disarmament East and West, including the tanks. For the people of Eastern Europe it doesn't make all that much difference whether the missiles come from the Atlantic or West Germany. There is just one point that is perhaps not adequately considered in the East: namely, that the stationing of the missiles here in West Germany will increase the danger of conflict breaking out in Europe. From the East the criticism is too much directed at the arming of the other side and not at the atomic danger itself. Although there is less talk about the possiblity of winning a nuclear war, there is a strong increase in militarism.

From our point of view the oppositional attitude to the tanks is correct, because in the final analysis the nuclear danger is engendered by the bloc confrontation. As I said after the coup in Poland, the Jaruzelski regime is a product not of Moscow alone but of both military blocs. An additional factor, which people there also see, is that the tanks are there not just to march against NATO but, as they did in the past, against Prague. However, we must also ask ourselves which is the most intelligent strategy to get rid of them. Is it more missiles in the West? Or is this not the method whereby Reagan simply strengthens Moscow's stranglehold on Eastern Europe? The discussion on these questions has already begun with the initiative of Thompson and the Russell Peace Foundation.

Can we now turn to the USSR itself and your assessment of Andropov? How do you see the perspectives for the Soviet Union in

the coming period in relation to both Eastern and Western Europe?
How will the Soviet Union react to the peace movement?

In what I say now, I am relying very much on some writings of Mlynař on the Soviet Union. My view is that the Soviet Union is overburdened by its role as world power, although paradoxically it was the bomb which allowed her to play this role in the first place. But from the point of view of the economy, the Soviet military machine is a clay-footed colossus. The leaders have certainly internalized this world-role, which is natural and sacred to them. Most of them were young officers in the Second World War and the military machine that Stalin mobilized against Hitler is for them the symbol of Soviet sovereignty. They know they can't be the victors in the economic rivalry with capitalism, and so they stick to the goal of military parity despite the burden it represents. In his last months Brezhnev restated the main dilemma facing the Soviet Union— military parity or the economy. And now Andropov is faced with the same dilemma. I believe he is a man with a more detailed and differentiated overview of the situation than Brezhnev. He was the spider in the web of information, and although he was also responsible for the repression of dissidents, his main preoccupation was the secret service. Obviously he has the subjective capacity to absorb and work on a vast quantity of information.

Both the American and the Soviet imperium have declined since the end of the war. They are losing their absolute hegemony in Europe which decided the basic shape of the post-war period, and I would say that Andropov belongs to the section of the Soviet leadership which realizes what is happening economically, militarily and socially. In view of the development of the scientific-technological revolution, there is a very serious risk that the Soviet Union will lose the arms race in the next ten or fifteen years. I don't think they will succeed in the field of electronic mass production. But if they do, as Castoriadis has suggested, it will be at the cost of a tremendous concentration in one sector which drains the rest of the economy in such a way that the whole system begins to fall apart.

I believe the Soviet leadership is heading for a very serious discussion of the option of isolationism, because they are already so overstretched and there is already the fear that they will lose the arms race. They will, of course, threaten to match every step taken by the West: their very weakness makes any retreat a subjectively unthinkable risk. But there is no question of any expansive tendency. They simply don't have the option of overrunning Western Europe. They must wish themselves relieved of the whole burden, and I believe that in the long run this will push them in the direction of withdrawal, of isolationism. Of course the forces engaged in the military sector would oppose this, and it remains to be seen how the internal discussion will develop. The Western peace movement, including supporters of a freeze and so on, will be an important factor in deciding the outcome of this discussion in the Soviet Union. If we don't succeed in stopping the missiles here, if American economic expansion successfully carries itself over into the military sphere and allows Washington to construct a defensive umbrella over the United States, then Moscow will be driven into a truly hopeless situation. I hope we will be able to convince a large enough section of European public opinion that it is in our own interest to facilitate a Soviet withdrawal from Eastern Europe.

This idea doesn't seem to have taken hold of the peace movement.

No. There is such an appalling dearth of strategic minds. Maybe this has to do with the fact that the eco-peace movement sees itself only as a protest movement, an opposition, a counter-force, instead of, as it were, the core of a new world order.

It's also true that questions of military strategy are always presented as questions of number. It is essential not just to avoid this kind of argument but to leave this particular battlefield altogether.

Yes. That is very typical. Many friends tell me that I shouldn't talk about Germany, that that is a dubious kind of nationalism.

Do you see a Soviet withdrawal from Eastern Europe as a strategic goal of the peace movement?

Yes, but not in the sense of a Soviet defeat. In fact, the long-term

Soviet goal, that Eastern Europe should be happy with the Soviet Union, has already ended in failure. In the final analysis even the GDR will be lost. However, since the Soviet Union cannot lose Eastern Europe to NATO, there must be an independent Western Europe. Some people then go on to talk of an armed, nuclear Europe, but that would be even worse than the present situation and goes completely against the logic of the peace movement. At the moment the Soviets fear the American missiles and don't really take the French or British seriously, but a third superpower in Europe would be a horrific perspective. The peace movement has to be won to a position of radical pacifism, total disarmament, our whole radical programme, so that at the level of general politics the politicians can be forced in the direction of defensive defence.

Your realistic goal, then, is defensive defence?

Yes. The power complex must be forced to go for a strategy of defensive defence that represents no threat to the Soviet Union.

But we are very far from that position now, both here and in the Soviet Union. I believe the Soviet Union is very suspicious of the peace movement here.

On the question of arms and disarmament, their position will always be to react to what happens in the West. The West has to make the first move. The conditions for this are much more favourable in Germany than they are in England or France because, as a result of the two world wars, any kind of expansionist military patriotism has no chance. The talk can only be about defence. Current military thinking would make Germany, and the whole of Europe, the battleground of the two superpowers. We therefore have some chance of splitting even the military elite on the question of the kind of defence we need.

Why, in your view, has the Sovet Union been so critical of the peace movement?

Whether we intend it or not, our conception of the dissolution of military blocs has an ideologically subversive function vis-à-vis Eastern Europe and it is seen as such by those who are unwilling to give up Eastern Europe without some realistic alternative perspective. So when I argue that the border should be opened to dialogue between the Eastern and Western peace movements, that is considered very disloyal towards the GDR. It really is an ambivalent situation, as was demonstrated by the fact that Honecker chose to ignore the subversive aspect of the action on Alexanderplatz in order to articulate a positive response to our disarmament proposals.

The role of the DKP *(West German Communist Party) is at least problematic. You have developed a thorough critique of the* DKP *and oppose cooperation with it. Indeed, whereas on international issues you have remained distinct from the anti-Soviet rhetoric in which much of the peace movement indulges, you have been militantly anti-Communist in international peace movement affairs.*

What the DKP is doing now is simply defending its own political and ideological existence. At one time, when there wasn't any other serious opposition to the system, there was always some brave Protestant pastor to demonstrate his independence by supporting the DKP. Such people now come to the Greens. If the DKP hasn't disappeared already, this is due to the fact that it is artificially kept alive by support from the GDR. It has a disproportionally large apparatus and about forty thousand members. But these are forty thousand activists—cadres who represent the interests of the Eastern bloc. Arguing that Soviet strength makes peace more secure, they defend parity and oppose the stationing of new missiles in Western Europe. In addition, they offer an ideologically confused explanation of the arms race in terms of the profit motive of Western capitalism. It's clear therefore that we can have no credibility as long as we are linked to the DKP. We can't win the argument here in terms of pro-Sovietism, but only by demonstrating our independence of both superpowers. We can't defend values with weapons that wipe out the people who have those values.

Are you against any minimal agreement or common front with the

Yes, not just for short-term but also for long-term reasons. The popular front policy of the thirties was an expression of the collapse of the labour movement, because it manipulated people to support a position which they did not essentially support. This basic conception can only lead to collapse because it does not allow a subjective formation around a particular historical perspective. The historical project of the DKP has already been proved a failure. Whether you say it collapsed with Liebknecht, the popular front or the cold war depends on how far back you want to go. But the model is finished and could only lead to a defeat for the peace movement. On the basis of this assessment I have said that the DKP doesn't belong to the peace movement, which is defined by its opposition to both blocs. Any policy which represents the interests of one bloc against the other has more to do with the preparation of war than with the struggle for peace. The DKP has as much to do with the peace movement as does Franz-Josef Strauss.

Did the nature and discipline of the DKP surprise you, by comparison with the SED? Is the CP here similar to the CP in the East?

I was less surprised than impressed, because it is such an absurd concept and I can only offer a social explanation for why it still holds together. With the material support of the GDR the DKP has created for itself a kind of habitat which gives it a certain stability. But in the GDR the Party has power: it draws to itself all those who want to advance, at the level either of career or of self-development, and who know that this can be done only through the Party. The formal consensus around the slogans of *Neues Deutschland* is very superficial and does not determine the daily life of people or their relations with the rest of society. For instance, when the technical director of a factory has to give the Mayday speech, this is just part of his job. He doesn't identify with what he is saying, and nor is he identified with it by others. He may be judged by how conspicuously or inconspicuously he has copied the speech from the lead article in *Neues Deutschland*. Since the SED is a ruling party, it must to a certain extent reflect the whole of the society. Here the DKP can only be a minority and, by its nature, a sect.

Do you also think that there is no place for the SPD in the peace movement?

I do. The peace movement, unlike the SPD, works with that part of the spectrum of consciousness, that part of psychic energy, which is not tied to the power complex. The SPD is part of that complex; it is by definition part of the NATO reserve in this country. Of course it's a different matter with individual Social Democrats, whether they are really part of the peace movement or merely a fig leaf for leadership policies. We can discuss with such people, confronting them with the fact that they merely spread the illusion of an SPD-inspired end to the arms race.

How do you see the future of the SPD in the competition with the Greens for the position of second main party? At one time you even went so far as to say that perhaps the Greens could find better allies in the CDU—in other words, a green-black rather than a green-red alliance.

That is an exaggeration. Within the established spectrum of the metropolitan power complex I make no fundamental distinction between the SPD and the CDU. When I argued that we must make the direct transition from black to green, this was directed against those who still argue the old front politics, who think that we have to put our policies in the container offered by the SPD. Our policies are compatible neither with the SPD nor with the CDU. In the red-green trajectory that has existed up to now within the forty-five per cent, we have simply tried to shift the ratio between ourselves and the SPD. But after this election a reform bloc with the SPD means no more than leaving the SPD to win back some voters from the CDU so that we can again try for fifty-one per cent. For me the strategic question is how to make the *direct* transition from black to green, bypassing the SPD and establishing a different relation of forces. The Greens were established during the period of the SPD-liberal coalition, and now it is necessary to break from the political conceptions which the Social Democrats sell to the workers and which are bound up with this reformist labour movement. The Social Democrats, not the CDU, can hold up the constitution of a distinctive green identity. Therefore the main attack has to be against the SPD.

Also against Eppler and the SPD Left?

Of course.

Is Eppler worse than Schmidt?

Yes. Of course he doesn't have worse policies on the arms race or ecology, but whereas Schmidt could never win people from the Greens to the SPD, Eppler could win people with his eco-reformist policies, could convince them to try once more with him. Then the whole thing would go on as before. So if it's necessary to constitute a new relation of forces, and if the people we want to win from the SPD have to be won to a completely different conception of politics, then we must first supplant the SPD as a political force. The end of the line has come for the whole reformist strategy of left versus right, whereby the job of the extreme left was always to strengthen and perhaps to radicalize a little the class fighters of the SPD. I never want to see the SPD in government again. It merely holds back the historical process. I see no reason why a worker who has this time voted CDU should ever be won back to the SPD. I look forward positively to the disintegration of the SPD, because it will set people free for a new political beginning. I think I can exert stronger pressure on the SPD from the outside. We must construct the discourse in such a way that they lose the conservative elements while the more open ones come to us. We thus cut up the SPD from both sides.

The paradigm of the workers' movement, this hundred-year-old social democracy, is nearing its end. There will be no new Godesberg. The SPD will not be able to reconstitute itself as an eco-reformist party, and any attempt to do so would only split it. If Eppler had left, he would probably have split the SPD. But he didn't leave, and I'm not so sure whether it was a good or a bad thing. For now we have an Eppler wing in the Greens.

Is the demise of the SPD a specifically German development? Or do you think it will be a general pattern for social democracy in the developed capitalist countries?

In this, as in all other things in the history of the European labour movement, German Social Democracy shows the way.

Do you think that socialism as a political concept is also finished?

This is similar to the problem we talked about earlier in respect to Marxism. If pushed hard, I couldn't deny that I am a utopian socialist because so many of the elements of utopian socialism appear in my commune perspective. But concepts are for doctoral dissertations and books. In reality socialism is what exists in Eastern Europe, or it is the practice of the French Socialist Party, the British Labour Party, or Craxi. It is also the theories defended by the left Social Democrats and the extreme left, the function of which is to cover up the actual practice of social democracy. So to this extent I am green and not red. The socialist concept, in theory and in practice, was tied to industrialism and statism. And since its theory is tied to the perspectives and historical practice of the disintegrating labour movement, it would be quite illogical for me to call myself a socialist. Like Marxism, socialism has become a quarry from which we can take various things, such as the concept of self-management which socialists have dropped in any case. The best and the permanent elements have been bequeathed to us.

There is a problem here with your strategy and your analysis of socialism. You say the workers' movement is finished. But although there has been no workers' revolution in the West and the labour movement is in crisis, it is undeniably true that we still live in a class society. Your strategy tries to deny or go around the fact that classes exist, that they are part of daily reality. In the long run I don't see how this is possible.

As I said before, I deny it only in the sense that I want to withdraw energy from the class conflict. If I discuss with a factory worker who wants to get involved in politics, I would advise him to invest one little finger of one hand in the trade union and to invest the rest in the new social movement. Trade union activity is a retrograde step. It's not good when Capital takes more than it should, but this whole defensive struggle takes place on a carousel which guarantees the continued reproduction of the system. Anyway, capital has an interest in stability and it won't go beyond certain limits. On the old front you can only reproduce the old hierarchy, the old crap, as Marx said. We must reproduce now only that which is needed as the infra-structure of a new society.

Would I be right in thinking that you see the transformation towards a new society not as a revolution but as an entropy of the old system. You speak of liberated zones, of communes. This transformation, if it comes, will take a very long time...

Before I speak of liberated zones in reality, I would speak of occupied and liberated areas of consciousness.

Is the socialist goal of common ownership of the means of production relevant any more?

No, not at national level. This in fact becomes part of my contraction perspective. Human appropriation of the earth as a whole has to happen, but I see this as a process of the reunification of people with their means of production and with the earth. The earth can belong to no one. But if I work on this piece of earth and take out no more than I need for simple reproduction, then I am the owner and the one responsible for passing it on to the next generation in an orderly way. The problem will no longer be one of expropriation but of appropriation—and appropriation only happens when concrete individuals really appropriate their conditions of life. The strange thing about expropriation in practice is that it has never led to appropriation.

At the end of the sixties, the SPD's Ostpolitik seemed to suggest the possibility that it would become independent of American foreign policy, if not actually neutral. In this perspective the theme emerged of a new Rapallo. You don't believe that the SPD could achieve that now. But could the Greens or another new government bring about a new Rapallo? What would that mean?

I have considered Rapallo as a perspective for the whole of Europe and not especially for Germany. Of course the inter-German dynamic would be a specific element in this. But the SPD's Ostpolitik is finished and, given its NATO connection, the possibility of a more radical foreign stance was never more than ideological speculation which nobody ever considered really relevant to power politics. The Greens, however, have from the very beginning constituted themselves outside of the bloc system. It is possible for us to talk about a German or European Rapallo, even at the risk of meeting with animosity in France. I have absolutely no sensitivity for the warnings of those militarists who say that we might damage Franco-German relations. They should test opinion in Alsace.

There seems to be a certain contradiction in your policy on the future of Germany. In the long run your perspective is to break up the national economy and the national state. That is your conscious goal, eco-communities and so on.

That's not explicitly in the programme, but it is somehow implied.

But when you speak of Germany's role as the catalyst of a new Europe, this seems to imply a strengthening, if not of nationalism, then of German national feeling. In the final analysis, are you not against nations?

I believe this to be one of those famous contradictions that exist in reality itself. It reminds me of what Marx said about the national constitution of the working class. In practice, if we want to build an ecological, decentralized Germany, we have first to free German territory. The Federal Republic is now under NATO and is the NATO country with the least sovereignty. For our perspective to work, we must first acquire sovereignty over our own territory. This inter-German border, which began as a foreign imposition and has become a danger-ridden frontier between the military blocs, only reminds the German people of the Bismarck state and the possibility of unity. It may be that the Germans would keep this border if they were ever given the chance to decide for themselves. I see no strong upsurge for reunification, at least not in the West. But the national question, including the possibility of reunification, must be discussed again, because only in this way can security and trust be created for the rest of the European people. I don't make any assumptions about what the Germans want. We know both types of situation well. In the Thirty Years War we had no central power and became the battlefield of Europe. Then came the German Reich and once more we were the battlefield of Europe. This is the national dilemma. Neither the presence nor the absence of a central state was the solution. Maybe the Germans would now come to the conclusion that things are not bad with the two German states, and perhaps that they would be even better if we had many smaller German states. This externally imposed border leads straight to a perspective of eco-communities. Still, there are several obstacles in the way: one is the presence in Germany of the two superpowers; another is the psychological barrier bound up with the externally imposed border itself. The Germans have to make a new breakthrough here. The eco-peace movement, which is preparing a discussion on this, is not a national movement in the sense of being defined in relation to national history. But it will become, among other things, a national movement. The question is not big Germany or little Germany. But the question of sovereignty or self-determination is, at this level, the key to everything.

Notes

Notes to Chapter One

[1]Kuba: pseudonym of the socialist writer Kurt Barthel (1914–1967), who spent the years 1933–45 in exile in England.

[2]Ehm Welk (1884–1966) was a socialist writer of novels and revolutionary dramas. *Die Heiden von Kummerow* (1937) describes from a schoolboy's viewpoint life in a Pomeranian village in the years leading up to 1914.

[3]El Campesino (Valentí González): legendary Communist leader of the People's Army during the Spanish Civil War. He later broke from the Communist movement.

[4]Eisenhüttenstadt-Ost was a mammoth enterprise, begun in 1950, to establish a steel complex on virgin territory around Fürstenberg-on-Oder. In 1961 Fürstenberg merged with the newly developed Stalinistadt to form the town that is now known as Eisenhüttenstadt.

[5]The 'National Committee for a Free Germany' was an anti-Hitler organization founded in 1943 in the Soviet Union and pledged to the destruction of Nazism and the establishment of a new state.

[6]*Wunschgetreu* = 'conformer'.

[7]*Lehr* = 'educational'; *leer* = 'empty'.

Titles of related interest from Verso

The Alternative in Eastern Europe
Rudolf Bahro

Exterminism and Cold War
E.P. Thompson and others

The Making of the Second Cold War
Fred Halliday

New Title – spring '84

The Politics of the Euromissiles
Europe's Place in America's World
Diana Johnstone